A Project Leader's to Recruitment and Selection

Appoint the best person for the role

Eddie Lunn

Alan Sarsby

Published by Spectaris Ltd.

Published 2015

A Project Leader's Guide to Recruitment and Selection

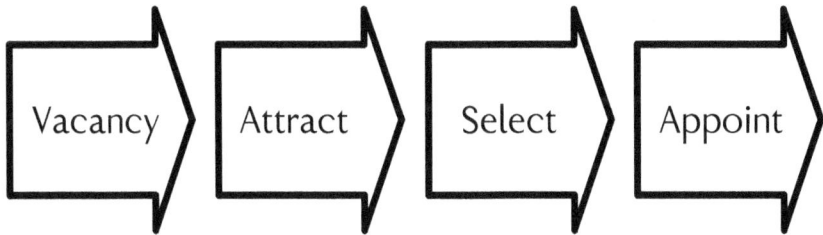

| Vacancy | Attract | Select | Appoint |

The leadership library

The leadership library is a collection of works addressing business activities from the standpoint that success is due to the balanced application of both leadership and managementship.

Leadership Library

First printing: 2015

Language <en-gb>

ISBN 978-0-9932504-0-8

The Leadership Library is an imprint of Spectaris Limited.
Registered in England: 05448422

www.leadership-library.co.uk

Preface

The terms leading and leader, and managing and manager, are often used interchangeably and this gives rise to confusion, or worse a focus on one to the detriment of the other. Having made the distinction, we should explain. Briefly, leader-ship and management-ship are different, complementary concepts.

Leader-ship

Leadership is primarily about leading and influencing people. Leadership is organic; it is the human aspect of work — it includes vision, values, the sense of purpose, and to bring meaning to activity. History provides many examples where leaders, by their words or deeds influence others to follow.

Leader-ship seeks answers to higher questions. It asks the 'why' questions: why is this important to us, why are we doing whatever it is that we do, why are we doing it this way, why do we need to recruit, why do we need to change? Leader-ship makes work meaningful.

Management-ship

Management-ship is primarily about realising the results. Management-ship is mechanistic: it is concerned with detailed tasks, using resources, implementing and monitoring plans, meeting delivery targets and deadlines. Management-ship is about managing processes.

Management-ship asks the 'what,' 'when,' and 'where' questions. What are we required to do? What is the budget? When do we need to do it by? Management-ship is concerned with efficiently of work.

> Note — the terms leader-ship and management-ship have been used to draw attention to the distinction. The remainder of this book now uses the terms leadership and management/managementship without the clumsy hyphenation.

Don't confuse the concepts of leadership and management with their use in job titles.

There is an extended version of the distinction between leadership and managementship on the leadership library web site at: www.leadership-library.co.uk

Contents

1   Leading recruitment

1.1   Begin with success in mind

If your recruitment need is simple and easily fulfilled by asking an agency to supply a suitable person — this guide is not for you. You might find some of the techniques interesting and ultimately useful. If the recruitment need is more about getting the right person in the right position to move your organisation along — this book helps you with approaches, project leadership, and the practicalities of recruitment and selection.

1.2   Success factors

Successful Recruitment and Selection is a combination of six success factors.

1) **The Approach.** Both leadership and managementship have their place in successful recruitment and selection, as does recognition that it is not a one-size-fits-all activity. Recruiting a senior executive is different from recruiting an operator, so a sense of proportion is important. A bias towards a strong management-ship and procedural approach can result in successfully hiring the wrong person, and over time, result in a leadership-scarce organisation that ultimately affects the culture and brand value of your business.

2) **The Role.** Producing and using a detailed and accurate role specification is more likely to ensure that the candidate selected and appointed meets the essential criteria and is a best-fit for the organisation.

3) **The Person.** A detailed and accurate person specification is more likely to ensure that the selected candidate is the best of those available to the organisation, and after appointment, you'll know what areas need to be developed further.

4) **The Method**. A well-crafted recruitment and selection method designed to attract, assess, and evaluate the candidates, is more likely to result in mutually best fit for both the candidate and the organisation. This guide includes several toolkits to help you design various parts of the overall method.

5) **The Project**. Organise the recruitment and selection activity professionally as a project with a designated project leader. Projects have vision, plans, goals, resources, and require communications; projects make it easier to:

- lead and manage the activity;
- monitor progress (re-focusing, if necessary);
- acquire the resources;
- align the assessment team;
- measure the return on your investment;
- review the completed results; and
- learn from the experience.

6) **A Focus on the Applicant**. Placing the applicant at the centre of your process with a balanced leadership and managementship approach is more likely to net the best available candidates, and a project-centred approach is more likely to make it happen.

> Recruitment can be expensive, but hiring the wrong person is considerably more.

2   Recruitment and Selection is a project

2.1   Benefits of a project approach

Recruitment and Selection starts with objectives and requirements, involves a series of activities, and aims to finish with a person or people appointed into the posts. The sequence of beginning-middle-end is one defining characteristic of a project.

There are several advantages to leading and managing recruitment and selection as a dedicated project, among these are:

1) The act of creating a Project Initiation Document, (PID), clarifies and defines the project and is used to gain authorisation for the recruitment project and the use of resources.

2) The definition of a governance structure that gives clarity to your colleagues, so they understand their role and responsibilities in your project.

3) The PID is a valuable communications tool both within and outside the project.

4) Treating Recruitment as a discrete and separate project distinguishes it from your business as usual schedule. By devoting dedicated time to oversee the project regularly, you can overcome delays or obstacles quickly and steer the project to a successful conclusion.

5) The use of basic project disciplines enables you to lead, monitor, and track progress to ensure success.

2.2 The three key project documents

The practice of project management is huge, so a sense of proportion is essential. Recruitment and selection is not a vast civil engineering job requiring everything that project management methodology like Prince2® has to offer, but a much simpler job requiring just three key documents, these are:

- **A Project Initiation Document**

  The Project Initiation Document, the PID*, states the purpose† of your recruitment and selection project, a summary of the business case, a scope statement, identifies roles and responsibilities, and commitment from those involved. The PID is a short document, typically between three and six pages.

  (*) In other project management regimes, the phrase *Terms of Reference* is used. The PID performs a similar role.

  (†) For example: *The purpose of this project is to recruit a production manager*

- **Project planning**

  The purpose of **planning** is to develop your thinking so that the various activities are well organised, done in the right sequence, and tested, so that everything happens. Effective planning can be achieved many ways, for example with sticky notes, or straightforward use of project planning software.

- **A business case**

  In many organisations, a business case is the document that when authorised, permits the consumption of resources. A business case supported by the PID and project plan, makes it clear that for an investment of time, resources, and money, the return on that investment is the right people are appointed to your organisation.

  The investment in resources adds up, and done well, recruitment can be an expensive activity

2.3 Project approach

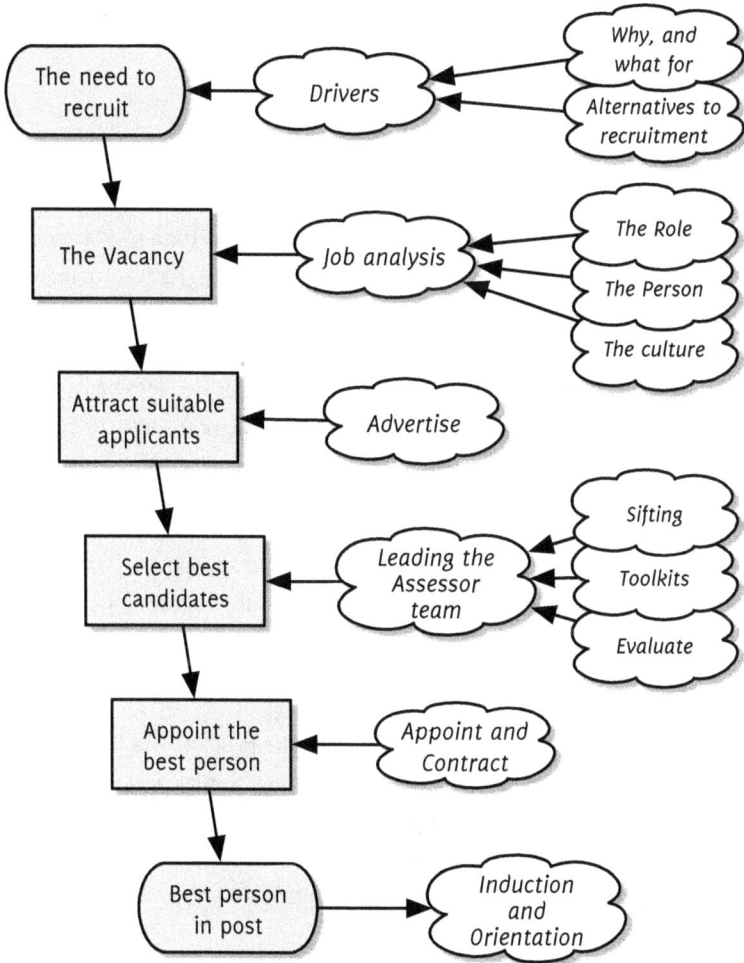

Figure 1 — Overview of the Recruitment and Selection approach

The six stages of the approach in Figure 1, or something similar, can be included in the PID. At this high-level view, it informs the project stakeholders that thought has been given to planning and hence how the recruitment and selection objective is to be met. It forms the basis of a more detailed working plan for the project team.

The purpose of each step is:

The Need to Recruit

Examining the need to recruit establishes the foundations for a recruitment project. This initial step involves asking the 'why' questions. For example, *why do we need more technicians? Why do we need a new IT director? Why is this role important to us, and why now?*

The need to recruit also examines the alternatives. Typically, these are 'what if' questions, for example: *What if we reorganise? What if we outsource the function?* And so on. Chapter 3 covers these issues.

The Vacancy

The activity at this step is to define what the role is, and what an ideal candidate might be. Two key parts define the vacancy or post: the role specification, and the person specification. Both are described in chapter 4.

Attract suitable candidates

Attracting candidates is the marketing aspect of the project. This includes the design of advertisements, the placement, and timing, so that potential candidates become aware of the opportunity. A well-designed advertisement encourages suitable people (and discourages the unsuitable) to apply for the vacancy. An approach to attracting the applicants is described in chapter 5.

Select the best candidates

Having encouraged suitable candidates to apply, you might now encounter the phenomenon known as the application avalanche (covered later). The objective is to reduce this avalanche to a workable number of suitable candidates. Then using a collection of methods, select those who best fit the role on offer. Selection is a non-trivial activity and is covered in chapters 6 to 9.

Appoint the best person

The penultimate step is to make a formal offer to the selected candidate(s). This is often done with an initial phone call to be followed up by a written formal job offer that confirms the details. This element includes due diligence (see chapter 12.2), an offer, and its acceptance.

If you've been timely, and in the meantime, your ideal candidate has not found other employment, then your recruitment and selection project is on-track to finish successfully.

Although the Recruitment and Selection project concludes with the appointment of the right person in post, there are two separate yet equally important activities to follow: Induction and orientation, and The Project Review.

Best person in post
The recruitment and selection project concludes when the newly appointed person arrives for their first day. The next step is induction and orientation: There are many activities to do on first day, during the first week, and the first month/quarter. These enable a new person in post to become familiar with how things work, is suitably trained, and begins contributing to the organisation. Induction and orientation are the responsibility of the new employee's line manager.

Project Review and closure
The most often missed-out part of any project is the post project review, or learning review. The purpose of this is to understand what when well, what caused problems, what can be kept for re-use, so that next time around it works even better. Project closure is covered in chapter 14.

Note:
Should your organisation have specific policies and procedures for the recruitment and selection, seek advice from your HR/Personnel advisor early in your project so it is aligned with corporate mandates.

3   The need to recruit

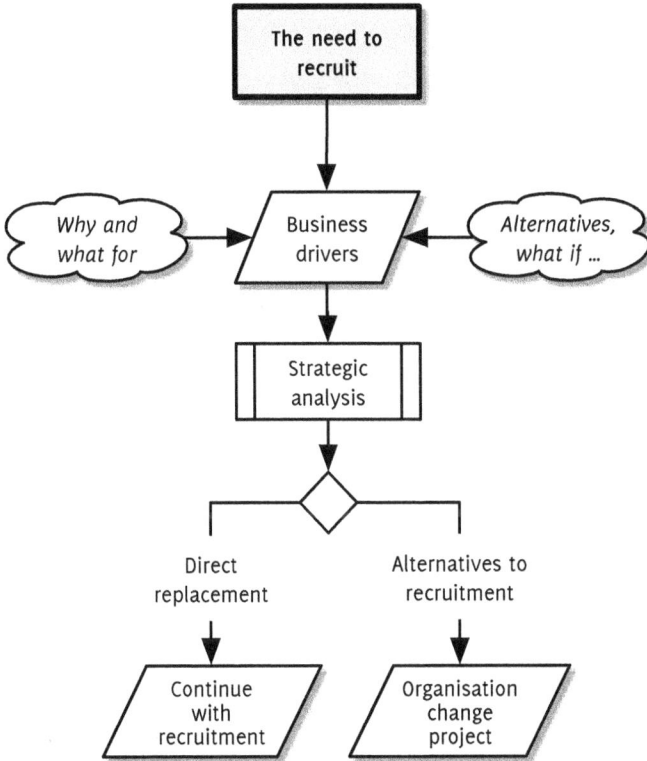

Figure 2 — Choices for Recruitment and Selection

3.1 Business drivers for recruitment

There are many reasons why you might need to recruit new people.

- Business expansion from increased sales, new products, or new markets.
- Existing employees leave to work elsewhere.
- Existing employees leave due to factors such as retirement, sick leave, or maternity leave.
- The business needs employees with new skills.
- Business relocation — and not all the existing workforce wants to move to the new location

Some situations are known in advance and can be planned. For example, retirement dates, planned expansion or product launch. Workforce planning is a valuable input to recruitment and selection. Other circumstances may be unforeseen or at short notice, for example illness, resignations.

This initial step in analysing the business drivers gives you the opportunity to consider the two main factors in deciding to recruit:

- Why do we need more technicians? Why do we need a new IT director? Why is this role important to us, and why now?
- What are the alternatives to recruitment?

3.2 Alternatives to recruitment

There are alternatives to recruitment: some of these include:

Reorganise — for example, if a supervisor leaves, it might be possible to share the workload amongst other supervisors, or transferring the responsibilities and work within the team.

Outsource — for example, take a critical look at the activity and consider whether it is distinctive to your business, or perhaps a common service that could be contracted-in. Strategic thinking tools can help with the analysis and decisions.

Workflow change — organisations suffer from inertia, and a workflow that might have been appropriate a decade earlier hasn't changed since. A change in people is always a catalyst for consideration of a change in workflow.

Any of these or similar decisions avoid the need for recruitment; instead, the rational and objectives then become the inputs to an organisational change project.

Table 1 — Comparing direct replacement versus larger changes

Direct replacement	Larger changes
To respond to an internal vacancy with a like-for-like replacement. To cover temporary periods, typically illness, jury service, maternity cover, or secondments. To maintain the workflow and capacity of a function. To respond to an external situation such as growth of existing product or service	To respond to changes in the external environment. To implement changes in products or services. To change workflows. To re-allocate the activity internally. To increase the capacity of a function. To introduce new talent or skills. To outsource non-critical functions.

Note:

Making larger changes require an organisation design activity with the inherent need for strategy analysis tools[*]. In this case, the organisation design is a parent project and the recruitment and selection is a sub-project.

(*) Strategy tools are covered elsewhere in the *Leadership Library*. Please check the website for current titles.

If your analysis results in a decision to recruit, proceed with the recruitment and selection project.

4   The Vacancy

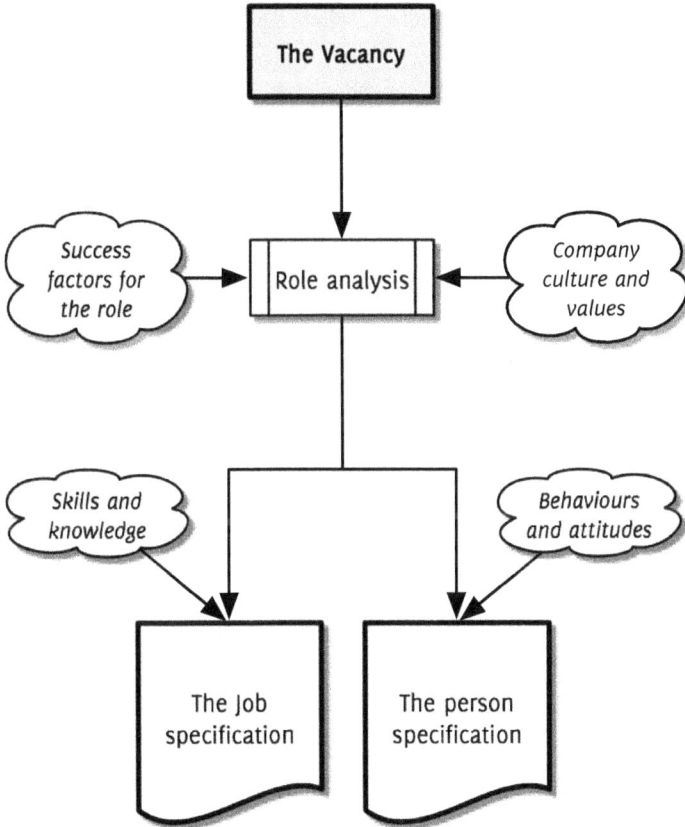

Figure 3 — Defining the vacancy

4.1 Separate the role from the person

A well-defined vacancy is the sum of two parts: a job specification and a person specification. The purpose of creating a specification for both the role and the person is to ensure that the recruitment planning and marketing are effective at attracting the interest of suitable candidates and equally effective at discouraging those who may be unsuitable.

- **The job specification**
  Is the functional definition of what the post-holder is there to do.

- **The person specification**
  Is the characteristics, attributes and behaviours, of the real individual that performs the functions that the post is there to achieve.

4.2 The role/job specification

The role/job specification is the functional aspects of the vacancy. It is primarily a managementship activity and best created by those close to the activity or the designer of the post in the case of larger changes.

The specification is a comprehensive list of criteria, when taken as a whole, defines the *function* of the role. The job specification includes:

- Where the job fits in with other functions, within the organisation, and the workflow.

- To whom the post-holder reports.

- The key activities or tasks that the post-holder is expected to complete.

- The outputs or targets, and to what standard.

- The educational, vocational, trade qualifications, or certifications, that is required to do the job. This includes registrations for legal or regulatory compliance.

- Requirements for on-the-job training.

- Required hours and attendance patterns.

- ... and others as required to perform the job.

Take care not to over-specify the role. For example, a functional requirement for being, say, fit able-bodied and a strong swimmer is relevant for a lifeguard; for a desk-based job, the ability to swim is irrelevant, and able-bodied is discriminatory.

4.3   The person specification

In contrast to the job specification, which is more process and function oriented (managementship), the person specification is more humanistic (leadership). The person specification includes behaviours, attitudes, and the soft-skills.

The person specification is a comprehensive list of criteria that an individual should have to be successful in the role. The person specification needs to be relevant and appropriate for the role, and not a grand wish list.

The person specification is the idealised form of the perfect candidate for the role. The person specification highlights those essential characteristics or behavioural traits that the individual needs to successful in the role.

The person specification could include factors such as:

- The ability to make the work meaningful and place it in context.
- Able to lead, inspire, motivate and influence others.
- High-level of self-awareness; seeks and offers effective feedback.
- Behaviours and attitudes, for example, 'attention to detail' or 'strategic thinker'.
- Relevant values consistent with the organisation or team. For example a commitment to customer service excellence, to quality, or to precision fabrication.
- Attitudes such as reliability, commitment, self-motivation, teamwork, persistence.
- The ability to communicate[*] to specific audiences[†]. For example, to conferences, shop floor teams, senior managers.

(*) Note: fluency in a language is a functional requirement and belongs in the job specification; delivering a compelling presentation is a personal (leadership) style and belongs in the person specification.

(†) Giving a presentation from the podium at an international audience of five hundred delegates is a different experience to that of a presenting the annual objectives at a team meeting of ten people. You should specify the types of audience that a candidate would need to address.

- Soft skills, for example: leadership of the team, resolving interpersonal conflicts, motivation of oneself and others, undertaking personal (one-to-one) reviews.
- Alignment with the core values of the organisation.
- Willing and able to be developed, trained, or mentored.
- Attitude to safety.
- Practical experience, a track record, past performance.
- The success criteria for the person appointed into the role.

It is likely that some items may appear on both the job specification and the person specification. Where this occurs it is essential to understand what differs between the role and the person doing the role.

4.4 Company culture and values

The Culture of an organisation means those things that are common in practice and taken for granted, for example, suits and ties for senior managers, dress-down Fridays, music in the workplace, and so on.

The Values of an organisation can be expressed in terms of how it is perceived and how it wants to be recognised. For example: consistent quality products, excellent customer service, reliable, accountability, and integrity in their customer-supplier relationships.

The Culture and Values of an organisation are an important consideration for sustainable success in the role. Ultimately your successful applicant is expected to have the skills, knowledge, and experience to fulfil the role; and the ability to 'fit in'.

4.5 Essential and desirable

Developing success criteria for the job and person specifications can result in a lengthy list that nobody matches. Too many criteria make it harder to recruit.

The most common way to organise and simplify each criterion is to separate them into two lists: *Essential* and *Desirable*.

- **Essential** — Criteria marked essential are those requirements that are required as the minimum to perform the role at an acceptable standard.

- **Desirable** — Criteria marked desirable are those requirements that enable the post holder to excel at the role or function and potentially contribute to the enhancement of the role.

Important note:
When crafting the person specification, take care to include only those criteria that are relevant to the performance of the role and that the specification is non-discriminatory. For example: age, sex, physical characteristics, marital status, religion and disability.

On-line information
The latest information regarding Employment Law can be found at:

- For the UK: http://www.legislation.gov.uk
- For the EU countries http://ec.europa.eu/
- For the United States of America http://www.dol.gov/

Nobody matches exactly every criterion in the job and person specifications.

4.6   Summary of typical requirements

Table 2 offers typical examples of the content of the job specification — the role and the person specification that enable an individual to perform the role successfully.

The role means what the organisation requires of the function (the post). The person specification means the skills, knowledge, behaviour, attitude, and values (the post holder).

Table 2 — Typical elements of the job/role and person specification

The role	The person
The context of the function in the organisation.	Context of the person and their characteristics in the role.
Purpose of the role: customer service, engineering, marketing, personnel, professional/technical or IT/technology, and so on.	Able to, and willing to, learn.
	The ability to give and receive feedback.
	Be reliable, responsible and committed.
Job title, job description, reporting lines,	Membership of (relevant) professional/learned societies.
Job-specific qualifications, licenses, or accreditations.	Demonstrable skills or practical experience.
Location, hours/shift patterns, salary and remuneration.	Ability to work on own initiative or in a team
Relationship to other roles functions, or departments.	Leading and managing self and others.
Key activities or tasks, achieve results to quality, time, and budget.	Ability to *lead* change.
Ability to *manage* change.	Ability to motivate self and others.
Production/product knowledge.	An effective communicator.
Requirements to manage operational issues. Development of operational plans.	

5   Marketing the vacancy

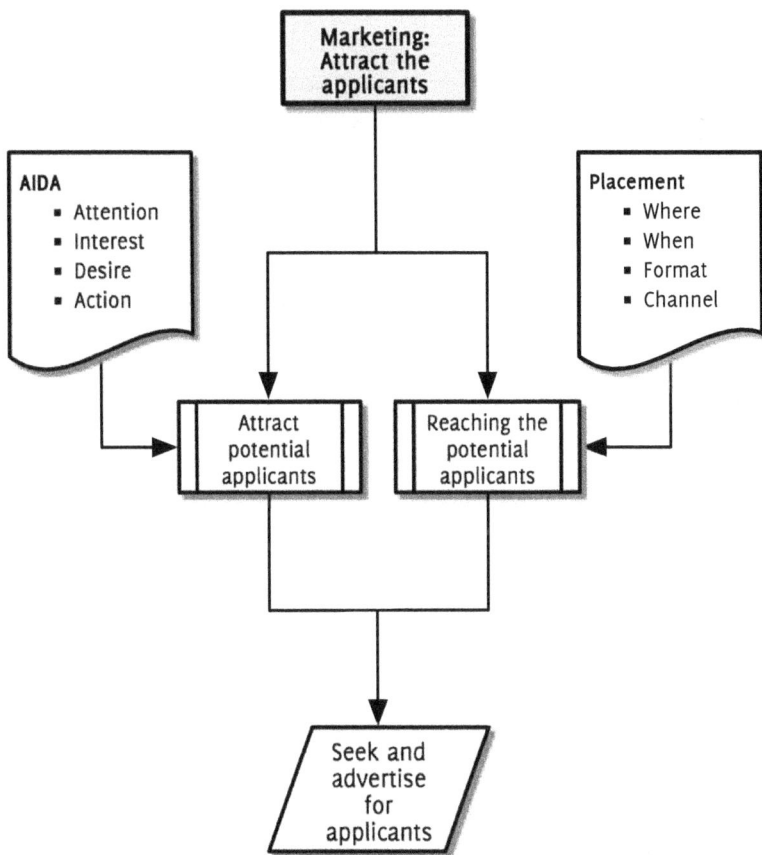

Figure 4 — Advertising for the right applicants

5.1 Attracting the right applicants

Effective marketing of your vacancy is essential in attracting and creating applicants for your vacancy. First, you have to gain their attention and then mobilise the interest such that the right applicants actually apply for your vacancy. A recognised and popular acronym in marketing is AIDA — Attention, Interest, Desire, and then Action.

Attention — The first part of AIDA is gaining Attention: how to gain the attention of suitable candidates? In practical terms, bold messages and statements are attention-grabbers especially if the advert is placed where it can be seen or heard by those individuals that you want to attract.

Interest — The advertisement should capture the interest of those applicants you want to attract while discouraging the unsuitable. The headline message should be relevant to the role and some substance behind it.

Desire — Ideally, as the applicant reads and gains an understanding of the opportunity. They gradually develop beyond the initial interest, and with increasing desire for the role form a picture of the job and importantly see themselves doing it. And then ... to take action...

Action — That part of the advertisement that indicates what to do next, typically this would include:

- How to apply, who to speak with, how to obtain an application form or submit their CV.
- The closing date — the date and time for receipt to qualify for consideration.
- An indication of when the applicant needs to be available for interview or assessment.

AIDA is a checklist and a guide — it helps focus on the key information and keeps it simple for the organisation and the applicants.

5.2 Designing the advert

The advertisement is predominately a visual communications medium. It is worth engaging a specialist who has skills in visual communications and graphic arts. A well-designed advertisement reflects positively on your brand.

The headline is the Attention statement. Its purpose is to gain the attention of the right kind of prospective applicants. Design the attention statement from the point of view of the people you want to attract and receive an application from. This element of AIDA should include the salary and benefits, travel, development, excitement, or enjoyment.

Other things to consider include:

- The layout and appearance says a great deal about your organisation, even if the potential applicant has not yet read a word. Use your branding elements precisely; for example, the corporate standard typeface (font), the logo, and other company marks. You'll need to include honest, representative, and convincing extracts from the job and person specifications. For the Action element of AIDA, make it unambiguous about what to do next.

- Language and style are part of the sales pitch. Use the language of the people you want to attract. Bold advertising seeking to recruit a creative thinker for a tightly controlled processing role is going to attract unsuitable applicants resulting in wasted time. Education-speak appeals to educationalists; seeking a mathematics teacher using maths speak is fine. On the other hand, if you want a head teacher to shake things up a bit, you'll attract the wrong candidates with a traditional style.

- Above all — the advert must be an authentic and honest reflection of the company and role. Advertising for a creative individual who then discovers the job has no place for imagination is going to resign shortly after being appointed. Then you have to do the whole thing again.

5.3 Checklist for a good advertisement

The effectiveness of advertisements can be tested using the job and person specifications. Together these create a pen picture of the ideal applicant so that you compare this ideal candidate against the advertisement.

Table 3 — Quality checklist for your advertisement

1	What is the attraction for a potential applicant, who may know nothing about your organisation? Why would the applicant take a risk and leave what they currently do and transfer their commitment to you and your organisation?
2	Is the type and context of the work expressed in terms that is likely to be attractive to the person who you want to recruit?
3	Does the advert appeal to the style of the individual imagined in the person specification?
4	Is there a match between the terminologies you use in the advert and the terminology used by the applicant? For example, a web designer understands HTML, CSS, DOM; a management accountant understands DCF and NPV. Using jargon filters-out those who are unsuitable, and adds exclusivity for those who understand the vocabulary — that is, the very people you want to attract.
5	Does the advert over-specify the ideal applicant? Asking for excessive qualifications, experience, and skills is going to deter some highly suitable applicants. Don't scare potential applicants at this point; near-miss applicants can be filtered out, or filtered in, later in the sifting stage.
6	Does the advert include the call-to-action information? How to apply? Dates for application? Who to telephone if the applicant wants to speak with someone?
7	Does the advert correctly use your corporate branding?

Note re item 4:
HTML HyperText Markup Language; CSS Cascading Style Sheets;
DOM Document Object Model
DCF Discounted Cash Flow; NPV Net Present Value.

A well-crafted job advert should enable people to self-select themselves into, or out of, your recruitment campaign, potentially saving you valuable time at the first selection phase of the process. The aim is to ensure that those who select themselves in at this stage are those you would want to hire!

Although it is not possible to consider all eventualities and situations within the job advert, anyone responding to your advert should not be surprised at the time of application, at the interview, or on recruitment, by anything included, or not included, in the advert.

A well crafted job advert attracts the suitable
and
discourages unsuitable applicants.

5.4 Advertising the vacancy

The decision to advertise externally is a significant and important investment. The three main considerations are:

Where the advertisement is placed. To borrow a technique from the world of sales, go to where your customers go. For recruitment, put the advert in a place where your perfect applicant is most likely to see it. Middle career people tend to read specialist trade journals. Candidates for more senior positions are likely to read the broadsheet papers or contact agencies for their next job.

What time of the year. The late summer and early autumn is often dominated with adverts for new graduates. The New Year is a good time for fulfilling resolutions; if you are looking for experienced people who want a new job, springtime is usually a good time to advertise. Trade journals have a calendar of topics* and features for forthcoming issues. These are often planned a year ahead and if your vacancy is somewhat specialist, an advertisement in a journal issue featuring that topic has a greater probability of being read by a suitable applicant.

(*) This information is often included in what is known as a *media pack*. Contact the journal and ask for a media pack. It usually includes the features calendar, the specifications for adverts (size & colour), pricing, and circulation details.

The size and colour of the advertisement. Advertising in journals and newspapers, is often priced according to size (column centimetres or page portions); colour is more expensive than black and white.

> The quality of the applicants follows the quality of the marketing.

5.5 Choosing the method of application

5.5.1 An application form or a CV?

The purpose of the application is to gather information from the applicant so that you filter the suitable from the unsuitable. In the main your choices are

An application form — a pre-formatted document with tick-boxes and spaces for prescribed and specific information.

A Curriculum Vitae — a document created by the applicant that states how they meet the job requirements, their employment history, and relevant information. It is the applicant's sales pitch for the vacancy.

Where a role has greater leadership requirements the CV is more likely to be relevant. For roles with a low level of managementship and a low level of leadership, a functional application form is more suitable.

There are occasions where both are required. One example is if your organisation is required by governing authorities to monitor, for example diversity. In that case, a tick-list document gathering only that specific data should be included as an addition, and separate from, the job application form or the curriculum vitae.

5.5.2 Using an application form

Application forms can be generic in nature or bespoke for a specific role. You might provide both to make it easy to process the generic details from the specific details. Applicants complete your application form by ticking Yes/No boxes, or writing a short response to a question seeking specific information.

The main benefit of requesting applicants complete an application form is that every applicant completes the same form enabling you to make an initial 'like-for-like' comparison. This makes it easier to perform the initial 'sift-in' of those applicants who appear to meet the needs of your vacancy and to 'sift-out' those applicants that do not sufficiently meet your criteria.

The major disadvantage of the dedicated application form is that it restricts the applicant to the information required on the form. This could mean that an applicant with valuable additional skills or knowledge could be missed.

When to use an application form

The advantage of an application form is that it collects only the information of interest you have requested. The use of application forms is most helpful where the role is well defined and/or involves a process-type activity where the skills and knowledge, outputs and targets are clear and generally well understood.

5.5.3 Using Curriculum Vitae

A curriculum vitae is the applicant's sales pitch for your vacancy. It enables the applicant to present a more personal and bespoke account of themselves. A curriculum vitae is an established method, especially for more senior positions. Typically, a curriculum vitae provides the applicant with a greater opportunity to highlight their career progression, qualifications, experience, and achievements.

A good applicant normally customises their curriculum vitae to match requirements you presented in the job and person specification. This enables both themselves and you, as their potential employer, to make an initial and easy judgement on their suitability for the role.

> Note:
> CVs are more difficult to judge like-for-like. No two applicants have the same life experiences so even similar competencies might be expressed in different ways. To sift a CV requires some extra time from you to read and interpret the content and match it to your specifications.

The key benefit of curriculum vitae is that you might discover additional potential beyond the scope of the specifications that the applicant can bring to the organisation. The main disadvantage is that the applicant might not provide some critical information or gloss over their shortcomings. The aim, as you process the curriculum vitae application, is to recognise how and where the applicant appears to meet your needs and those of your organisation.

Note the layout and presentation of the information and the language or terminology used; you may also detect some information that appears to conflict with your needs and those of the organisation, and facts that need to be confirmed at interview. Compare and contrast against your agreed criteria for success in the role.

When to request a CV application

The flexibility of the curriculum vitae is helpful where the job role is less well defined and there is greater scope for creativity, or initiative.

Table 4 — Typical factors influencing the choice for a CV or an application form

Curriculum Vitae	Application Form
Loose, flexible, adaptive or creative type role. New creative roles — where Vision or Creativity is required. Strategic Planning, developing new products or new work streams. Organisational Leadership. Senior roles and Director positions, High leadership needs	Tightly controlled, non-adaptive, inflexible type processing type role, for example administrative role, data processing. Fixed or repetitive process. Managed script or output Production Assistant, Process controller, Book keeping, Inventory control, Call Centre agent

5.6 Inviting responses

The final element of AIDA is Action — what do you want the applicant to do next? Some options are:

Ask the applicant to phone in — so you can tell them more than there was space for in the advertisement. You can make some preliminary assessments on basic matters, and encourage or discourage their interest.

Ask the applicants to request (or download) an information pack — an information pack should, at least, contain some company information, the job and person specifications, and other forms (some organisations require certain compliance monitoring data to be recorded).

How to apply — whether this is by completing an application form (on paper or on screen), or by submitting curriculum vitae? See chapter 5.5.

When to apply — if you have a deadline, make sure it is easy to see and unambiguous. A date presented as 9am, Monday 25 November 2015 is precise and unambiguous.

Remember that the experience an applicant encounters, at any stage of the recruitment project influences their assumption of how your organisation behaves; it is their experience of your brand.

As a rule of thumb, you should make it easy for the applicants to apply. That means clear communications and precise instructions, easy navigation to the up-to-date part of a web site, and correct files and forms available for download.

> Make it easy for good
> candidates to apply.

6 Sifting through the avalanche

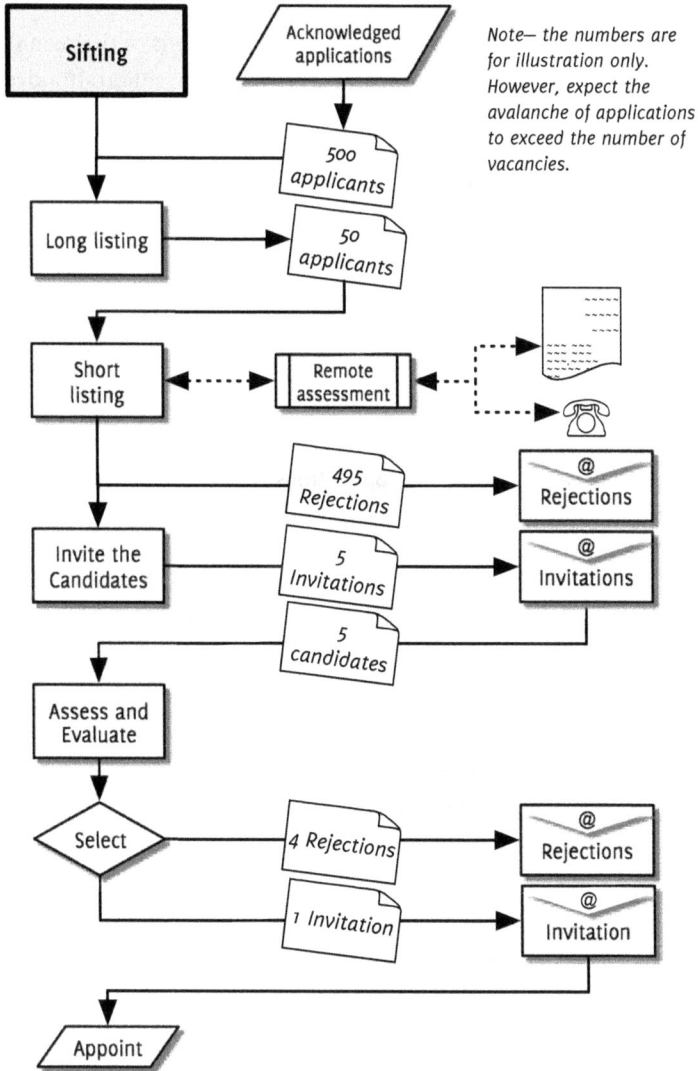

Note— the numbers are for illustration only. However, expect the avalanche of applications to exceed the number of vacancies.

Figure 5 — Sifting the avalanche of applications to the likely few.

6.1   Sifting the avalanche of applications

6.1.1   The aim of sifting

The aim of sifting is to reduce the number of applicants to about five candidates per vacancy who are then invited to an assessment.

You have reached your target audience and sown the seeds of desire in your potential applicants. The advert is successful and the applications flood in!

Expect to receive many more applications than there are vacancies. This ratio can be very high with one-hundred to five-hundred applicants per vacancy being a common response rate. Having invited applications, you have also set expectations that the recruitment timetable is going to progress in an orderly and swift way. If it doesn't you can reasonably expect the applicants to express negative opinions about your organisation, then to devote their attentions elsewhere. This is brand damage.

6.1.2   Resourcing the sift — A Worked example

If you assume an avalanche of 500 applications for one vacancy, the purpose of the first sift is to reduce the number to approximately 50.

500 applications × 2 minutes (average each) = 1000 minutes
    = approximately 17 hours work + 1 hour setup and admin = 18 hours
assuming a nett 6 working hours per day
    = approximately 3 project workdays.
Assuming a reviewer has 70% utilisation of their working time,
3 project workdays ÷ 0.7 utilisation = 4 elapsed days
(minimum, there might be interruptions that extend the elapsed days).

> Note 1:
> The two minutes per application in the first sift is a generous allocation. With the other elements of an application (cover letter, monitoring forms, and so on) it is easy to see where the adage that a CV has just 30 seconds to make an impact. Sifting is resource hungry!

> Note 2:
> Where an agency performs the first sift, the number of applications you receive is the reduced number.

6.1.3 Death valley

In sales, there is a period between making the pitch and learning the outcome; it is often called Death Valley. From the perspective of your applicant, this is the period between submitting an application and hearing some news. It is a period of high-stress for the candidate and high-risk for you. A good candidate is likely to be pursuing other opportunities so an overly long wait between communications might mean a good candidate has found a role elsewhere — keep the death valley period as short as possible.

You need a management system in place to:

Acknowledge applications — a simple 'thank you for your application ...'

Manage the expectations of the applicants — so that they are clear about what happens next and when.

- How long does the process take from application to interview?
- When and where the interviews or the assessments take place?
- Are any tests or a telephone interview involved?
- What is the intended start date?
- When further contact might occur, and so on.

6.2   Filter in — Filter out

6.2.1   Introduction to filtering

It is normal to receive many more applications than there are vacancies. So the first activity is to filter-in and filter-out to reduce the volume of applications to a feasible number. This stage is commonly known as the paper-sift, the essence of which is to compare and match the information in the application with the job specification and the person specification. Depending on the number of applicants there may be a need to repeat the process using a progressively finer filtering.

In addition to reading and reviewing each application, you'll also need a tracking method, for example a document or spreadsheet that contains a record of the of the review. In particular how well each application meets the specifications, and to record the decision for the next step.

Note:
    This tracking documentation is essential if an applicant subsequently makes any claim of unfair treatment.

6.2.2 Principles of filtering

The principle of filtering is the degree to which the application matches the job and person specifications; there are four possible cases:

Matches both the job and person specifications:
The ideal application indicates how well the potential candidate could fit with the organisation and that they have the essential skills, knowledge and experience to undertake the role successfully.

A good match with the person specification only:
An application that is a good match with the person specification, yet a poor match with the job specification indicates that the potential candidate could fit within the organisation dependent upon the complexity of the role and how much training and development they might require.

A good match with the job specification only:
An application that is a poor match with the person specification yet a good match with the job specification indicates that the potential candidate might be able to undertake the role successfully dependent on their integration into the organisation.

A poor match with both specifications:
An application that is a poor fit with both the job specification and the person specification means the applicant is unlikely to survive an initial paper-sift

6.3   Long-listing

The first sift uses a coarse filter that essentially separates those applications that broadly meets the requirements from those that don't. Typically, this long-listing activity reduces the avalanche to one-tenth. The example of 500 applications would become 50 applicants progressing to the next stage in readiness for a further round of review to create a short list.

> Note:
> A short questionnaire can be designed and used as a coarse filter to differentiate applicants. This can be used to establish specific values, behaviours or organisational fit (ethics, behaviours, attitudes).

You might want to involve someone not directly connected to the role in this initial paper-sift to provide a degree of independence. The individual or individuals you select to conduct the long-listing process should be able to suspend any emotional connection with either the person or the role.

> Note:
> A complementary option to the paper-sifting process could include a telephone interview. The use of a short telephone interview is a valuable sifting method where it is desirable yet impractical to have a large number of face-to-face interviews.

6.4   Short-listing

To create a shortlist from the long list follow the same principles by examining the application and testing the applicant's match to the job and person specifications in more depth, i.e. using the essential criteria, and progressively more of the desirable criteria. At this stage, you might also identify and note particularly interesting features of the application that could enhance the role.

The short-listed applicants become your list of candidates to be invited for interview or assessment.

You have the opportunity to make the sifting more scientific by assigning scores or weighting to the various factors in each specification. The assigned weighting factors should highlight the more important criteria for success from the less important. (There is more about weighting in chapter 9.3.)

An overly procedural sift has a bias to managementship and an aversion to the softer, more difficult to quantify, leadership qualities, which can successfully sift out good applicants if you let it.

The result of a successful paper sift is that all suitable applicants are in one pile, and the unsuitable in a separate pile. The converse is also true — that a suitable applicant hasn't been missed, and an unsuitable applicant has not been progressed.

Procedures can be biased, don't let them make your decisions.

6.5   Invitations

A personal invitation followed by written confirmation is an effective method for gaining or assessing commitment, prior to the interview. It also presents an opportunity for you to lead and manage the expectations of the applicant by:

- Confirming the date, time, and duration of the interview or assessment.

- Outlining what the candidate should expect to happen on the day. For example, interviews, ability tests, presentations, or other assignments. You should also indicate how these are to be used in the evaluations and what happens to the data afterwards.

- Indicating the timescale for follow-up and notifying the successful candidate.

- Indicating if there is an opportunity to look round, talk to other employees, or discuss any other points, in advance or during their visit.

Always advise your candidates of any delays so that you engage and retain their interest. During a recruitment and selection project, no news is bad news. Good people and possibly the best available candidates have other opportunities open to them and elect to join other organisations while waiting to hear of progress from you. A delay in Human Resources processing is a serious risk. Good project timekeeping is vital to avoid the risks of 'death valley'.

6.6   Rejection letters

For apparently legal reasons (perhaps, fearful of litigation) rejection letters tend to be short, perfunctory, and almost without content or human feelings. This is a shame because even in a short correspondence there are elements that can be included to give your applicant something to speak positively about with their friends and colleagues.

Suitably crafted rejection letters can go along way to maintaining or enhancing your image, brand and reputation.

- Wherever practical and possible rejection letters should be addressed correctly and personally, NEVER to *Dear applicant*.

- Thank the applicant for their application, interest and time, when this is phrased in genuine terms; it conveys the message that your organisation is courteous and caring.

- Mention how many applications were received. The applicant can then use that number in their conversations. If you use this approach, the number should be broadly accurate. *There were five hundred applications for the xyz job.*

- Avoid crass phrases such as *the standard of applicants was high* — it just reinforces that the applicant didn't reach the standard. The intent, for you and the organisation is that it should convey that your organisation is a popular and attractive place to work.

- Depending on your plans, it can be appropriate to ask the applicant if they agree that you retain their application details or CV on file for future opportunities.

> Consider the impact of 499 high quality rejection letters, versus the brand damage of silence.

7 Assessment design principles

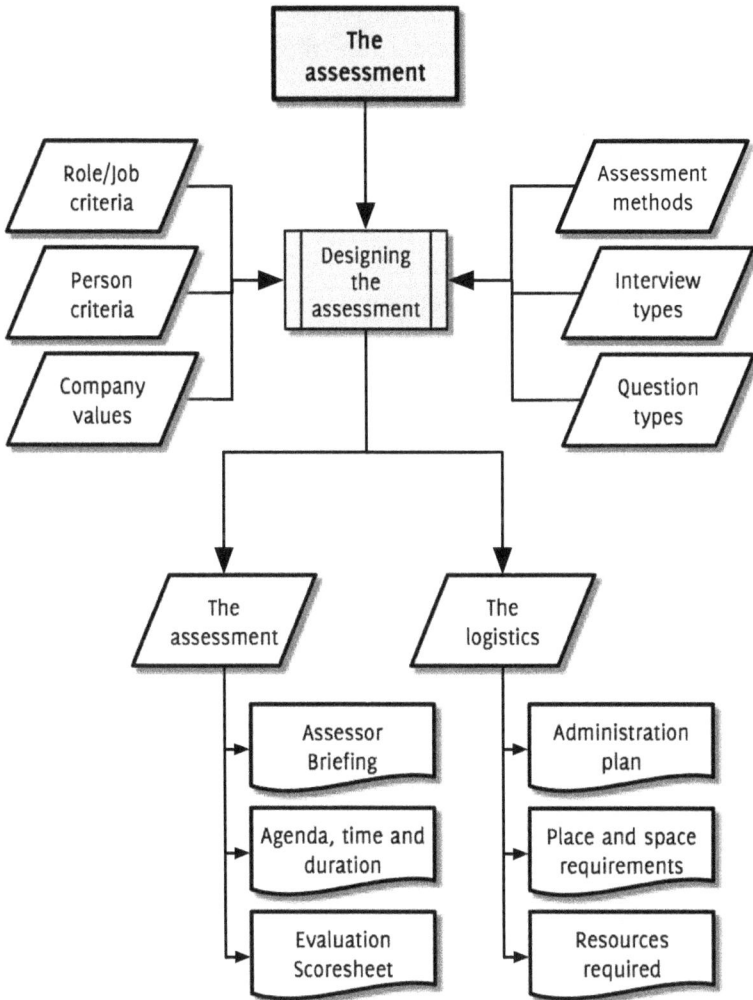

Figure 6 — Outline of Assessment design

7.1 The purpose of assessments

At the end of the paper-sift stage, you have a short-list of candidates, and at least on paper, all could fill the vacancy. However, you don't know how accurate the information is on the application form or CV. Hence, the purpose of an assessment stage is two-fold: to verify to your satisfaction that the candidate's claims are substantive, and to further differentiate among the candidates so you can select and appoint specific individuals.

7.2 Design principles for assessments

The overarching design principle is:

> To design an assessment that links the job and person specifications, to one or more activities, which enables a candidate to display their skills and competence in those specifications, in such a way that it can be observed, recorded, and then evaluated.

The objective in designing the assessment is to maximise the effectiveness of the assessment by acquiring actual evidence of the capability of each candidate.

In summary, the important parts are:

- The job and person specifications.
- Linkage to an activity/activities that are observed and assessed.
- Design evaluation into the activity from the outset.
- The administration/logistics plan is important so everyone is in the right place at the right time.

The six main inputs to the assessment are shown in Figure 6. From these, the job of the design activity is to decide what methods of assessment are most effective to help you verify and differentiate among the candidates.

Typically, an assessment consists of many activities — all need designing so they work together and fulfil the dual objectives of verification and differentiation.

A second design principle is to align the depth and intensity of the assessment with the level of the vacancy. The risk associated with hiring a production operator is much lower than the risk of hiring a head-of-department; therefore devote more resources where the risk is higher.

Be aware that a more thorough assessment requires more time for planning and preparation, and consequently budget and resources.

7.3 Choices for assessment activities

7.3.1 Individual or group assessments

Assessments are activities of some kind. Generally, the assessment activity falls into two categories (inevitably, with some overlap): Individual assessments, and group (or team) assessments.

Table 5 — Contrasting individual and group assessments

Individual assessments	Group assessments
• Interviews	• Group conversations/interactions
• Individual presentation	• Group presentation
• Ability tests (for example, time-management, decision-making, knowledge, skills/trade-tests, planning and organising)	• Group problem solving (for example, teamwork, using each other's skills/knowledge, collaboration, sharing workload)
• Individual assignments and problem solving	• Group assignments or problem solving

There is value in selecting more than one assessment activity. For example an interview[*] and a complementary ability test enable a candidate to demonstrate their skills and competencies in different situations so that you can corroborate the evidence.

(*) It is rare that an assessment does not include at least one face-to-face interview.

7.3.2 Individual assessments

An individual assessment is where a single candidate is assessed without the presence of other candidates. Individual assessments include, for example:

Interviews — Interviews are the most common form of assessment activity. Interviews range from one-to-one (a single candidate to single interviewer), to one-to-many (a single candidate to an interview panel).

Ability tests — An ability test where the candidate alone undertakes some prescribed activity without help or input from other candidates.

The benefits of individual assessments enable:

- Candidates to give their best if they want to share their knowledge only with you, and not share it with competing candidates.

- The assessors to pursue a specific point to a single candidate without wasting the time of others.

- Introverted[*] candidates to give their best without being shouted-out by the extroverts.

    (*) Remember that Introversion and Shyness are different. Introversion as a preference is a Think-Do-Think cycle of action. Extroverts follow a cycle of Do-Think-Do (in speech, it is talk-think-talk). As an observer, be aware that the introverts 'think' time might be overwhelmed by the extroverts 'talk' time. Shyness is the fear of being unfairly judged (often by judgemental people in a position of authority).

7.3.3 Group assessments

A group assessment is where candidates are assessed simultaneously in the presence of other candidates. Remember that each candidate is being assessed as an individual within a group context. Group activities could include:

Team working — For example, solving a puzzle or problem by a group of candidates. These need to be overseen by a competent facilitator and watched by skilled observers to identify skills, knowledge and behaviours that might not be evident from an interview alone.

Social interviews — Sometimes called 'trial by sherry', where the candidates are invited to a getting-to-know you event or a dinner during which they are 'tempted' to reveal more about themselves in a relaxed environment. Exercise extreme care if this option is part of your Recruitment and Selection project.

> Note:
> The potentially subversive nature of a social interview can leave you open to challenges of unfairness (extroverts may come out better than introverts — but both could do the job). In a similar way, disguised interviewing, for example, during a factory tour, is unacceptable.

A group conversations and interactions — For example a topic (such as a business, operational, or current affairs situation) is given to the group of candidates as the subject for a group discussion. A facilitator or moderator takes a leading role and asks questions of the group or individuals. Observers look for and record the candidates' skills, knowledge, and group oriented behaviours (for example, inviting others to join in, or building on other's ideas).

The benefits of group assessments include:

- The opportunity to observe how candidates work and interact in a group context. If your corporate values include something along the lines of *we work as one team*' then a team-based activity is relevant.

- To observe the strengths of each candidate when working together. For example, the candidates who are the natural planners, the natural organiser, the natural leader (but you need to be clear what a leader is). Which candidates are creative or willing to experiment, and which are the communicators or persuaders. Remember that the competencies you are looking for are those in the job and person specifications.

Note:
> The observers need to distinguish between real team-workers, and 'look-at-me' candidates. Remember, this is an artificial environment that favours talkative candidates.

7.4   Assessment logistics

Where is the assessment conducted?
Most assessment activity is conducted at a physical location chosen by the Project Leader. Some assessment activity may depend on the availability of specialist people and there may be options to conduct some testing or questionnaires on-line prior to interview.

How long should be allocated for each individual or group assessment?
Time allocation can be tricky, however each candidate should have the same time opportunity for the same activity.

For example: the time allocation for a business case analysis and presentation could be: a 10 minute briefing to the candidate, 1 hour for the candidate to analyse and prepare; a 20 minute time-slot for a 15 minute presentation, and 20 minutes for a Question and Answer session. Total time = 1 hour 50 minutes; an overall time-slot of two hours is prudent.

Remember to include time for the candidates to have a rest-break, movement between rooms and to set up activities. The assessment team also need time to review their notes and to have rest breaks.

What resources, including people, are required to introduce the assessment, record the event and evaluate the results?
Business simulations may need to be compiled, skill tests established, or ability tests purchased. The assessment team could consist of: administrators, test practitioners, observers/assessors, interviewers, note-takers some of whom may need training depending on their role in the assessment process.

An Administration plan includes the agenda, locations, the timings, roles, briefings and documents for all those involved in the assessment. Briefings should cover all aspects of the assessment to provide contingency for the Project Leader should they need it.

It may be prudent to select some volunteers from the organisation to act as pseudo-candidates. They can benefit from experiencing the process in readiness for future roles, or career development.

8   Assessment design toolkit

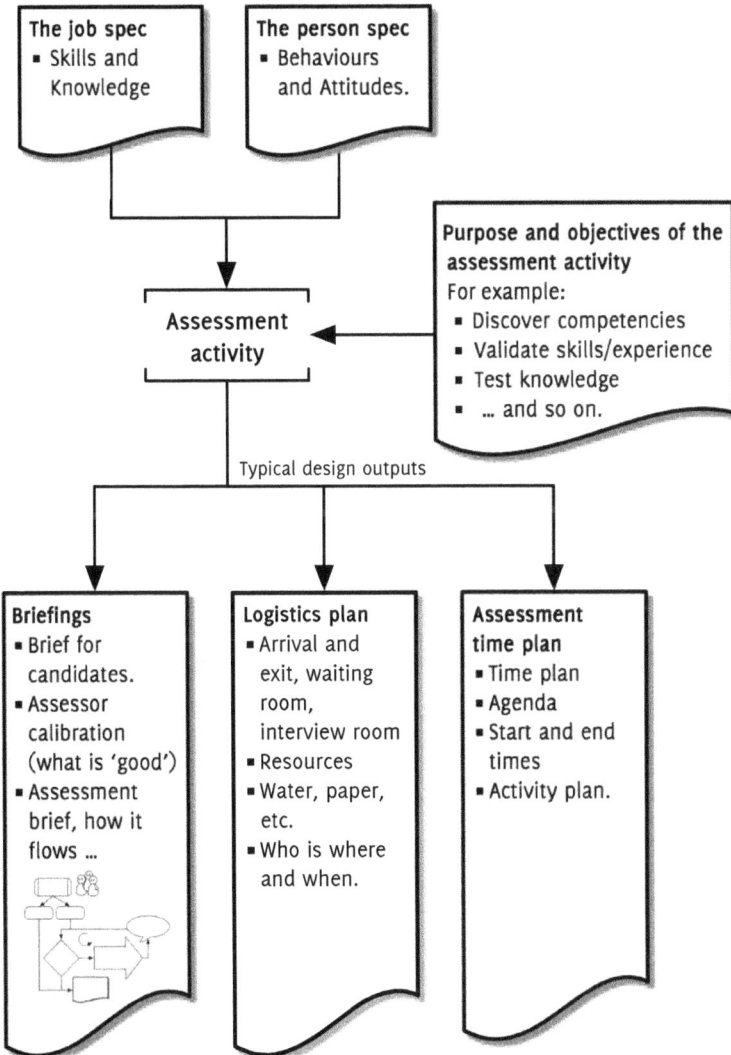

The job spec
- Skills and Knowledge

The person spec
- Behaviours and Attitudes.

Assessment activity

Purpose and objectives of the assessment activity

For example:
- Discover competencies
- Validate skills/experience
- Test knowledge
- ... and so on.

Typical design outputs

Briefings
- Brief for candidates.
- Assessor calibration (what is 'good')
- Assessment brief, how it flows ...

Logistics plan
- Arrival and exit, waiting room, interview room
- Resources
- Water, paper, etc.
- Who is where and when.

Assessment time plan
- Time plan
- Agenda
- Start and end times
- Activity plan.

Figure 7: Template for assessment design

8.1 Objectives of the toolkit

Figure 7 shows the overall design template. The purpose of this chapter is to introduce a range of tools you can use to create real documents and activities to support the assessment objectives.

All assessment activities share some common design objectives. These are:

Linking — Link the assessment activity to the job and role specifications. This makes it easier align the subsequent observation with the competencies you are interested in. For the candidate, it makes the assessment activity relevant to the vacancy.

Expectations — Design the briefings (spoken and written) so that they lead and manage the expectations of both the candidate and the assessors. The briefings should put your candidate(s) at ease so they can give their best performance.

Clarity — The entire project team, and those in ancillary roles, need to be clear about their part. For the candidate it must be clear what you are asking them to do.

Assessable — Design the activity so that assessors and observers can assess the activities.

Timing — Ensure the assessment can be achieved within the given time.

8.2   The toolkit for questions

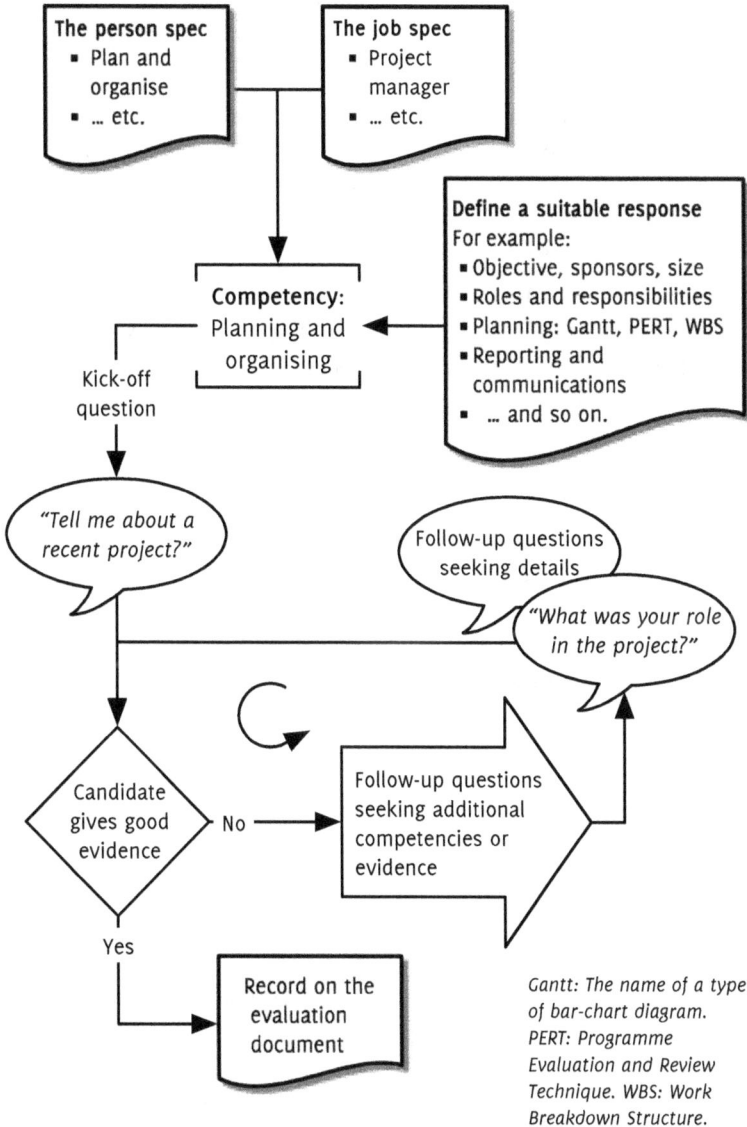

The person spec	The job spec
▪ Plan and organise	▪ Project manager
▪ … etc.	▪ … etc.

Define a suitable response
For example:
- Objective, sponsors, size
- Roles and responsibilities
- Planning: Gantt, PERT, WBS
- Reporting and communications
- … and so on.

Competency:
Planning and organising

Kick-off question

"Tell me about a recent project?"

Follow-up questions seeking details

"What was your role in the project?"

Candidate gives good evidence

No → Follow-up questions seeking additional competencies or evidence

Yes

Record on the evaluation document

Gantt: The name of a type of bar-chart diagram. PERT: Programme Evaluation and Review Technique. WBS: Work Breakdown Structure.

Figure 8 — Example: Linking questions to competencies

8.2.1 The role of questions in assessing

The purpose of the questions is to invite the candidate to give evidence you can match to the competencies. Questions come in many guises and are used to discover specific competencies, to seek knowledge, or test for behaviours. Your role as project leader is to prepare questions that enable a candidate to demonstrate how they meet the criteria. Questions are used in many activities: interviews, presentations, and ability tests. Questions are at the core of assessments.

8.2.2 Design goals for assessment questions

Questions come in many formats: the main classifications are open and closed. The intermediate formats are directing (partially open), and leading (partially closed). All, except leading questions, have a use in assessing — the objective is to design a question that elicits specific information from the candidate. Question formats vary depending on what you are assessing.

The toolkit for high-quality questions for use in assessing includes:

Link questions to the specifications

Basing the questions on the job and person specifications ensures that every question helps both the candidate give a relevant answer, and because of this, you can record clear evidence against the competencies.

> Note:
> The candidate's response might give evidence for several competencies, if so you have corroboration. It might be the case that evidence for all the competencies is delivered in one theme of questioning, in which case you can omit some of the remaining prepared questions.

Form and structure of questions

The classic 5 Ws, and 1 H, are foundation of most questions, these are: Why ..., What ..., Where ..., When ..., Who ..., How ....

Others include 'Tell ...', 'Explain ...', and 'Describe ...'. Each of these can be combined with 'precisely', 'in detail', and 'exactly' to direct the candidate towards the information you are seeking.

Phrase the question to the candidate

Phrase questions with the candidate as the subject, *you* or *your*. This helps to keep the assessment focused on the candidate. Table 6 illustrates the types of questions with examples of how they are used in an interview.

Clarity — one question at once

You might be familiar with radio and television chat show hosts who ask their guests multiple questions at once. For example, *"So you have an new film due soon, how was it working with the director, what was your leading lady like, did you have fun on set?"* Here, the host has made one statement and asked three questions within a single sentence.

Multipoint questioning is unsuitable for assessment because the candidate is likely to answer only the first, or only the last, question and forget the others. It also conditions the candidate to give short answers from which you cannot gather substantive evidence. The adage, Keep it Simple is a good design objective for assessment questions. The design goal is one question at once.

> Note:
> A smart candidate is likely to intercept multipoint questions and throw it back at you. It can make you look foolish and attract a poor reputation in the eyes of the candidate (brand damage), and the other assessors (loss of personal reputation).

Ask questions in a positive tone without a negative modifier

Questions with negative modifiers are a source of much confusion. An assessment interview is not the place for confusion so negative modifiers are to be avoided.

A question with a negative modifier such as: *"Are you not coming to the football match?"* might be answered by your candidate in two ways: according to the embedded fact, or according to the logic of the whole statement.

- Answering 'yes' according to the fact means that the candidate **is** going to the match.

- An answer 'yes' according to logic means the statement is correct and the candidate **is not** going to match.

Your problem is that receiving a 'yes' answer has two different and opposite meanings is that you don't know which one the candidate meant. This makes it difficult to pursue follow up questions and gather evidence for the assessment.

If you encounter a candidate answering using a full sentence such as *"Yes, I am not."* it is a good clue that the candidate is suffering an internal conflict between the embedded facts and the logic of your question.

> Note:
> You might receive the same, logically correct, negative-yes ('yes, I am not') from computer scientists, engineers, and others who are skilled in the mathematics of logic. Students of philosophy are also likely to answer according to logic.

Asking questions using positive terms avoids the confusion.

The critical few questions

In the design phase, it is tempting and easy to develop a lengthy list of questions. A long list of questions has a tendency force an assessor into a scattergun approach, and in turn, can let the candidate form an opinion that it the assessment is a trip-me-up, catch-me-out approach. From the long-list of questions, reduce these to the critical few. These include:

- The role specific questions that enable the candidate to give their best; and

- The few standard questions that you must ask all candidates for compliance reasons.

Do not ask a question because it is on the list — ask it because it can gather information, clarify, or to corroborate a point the candidate made previously.

Table 6 — A toolkit of question types used in assessing

Question objective	Examples	When to use
Warm-up	How far have you travelled today? Have you had some refreshments? What have you brought with you?	Establish rapport — early engagement. Use as warm-up questions where the answers are simple and safe. Initial fact-finding.
Topic	Tell me about your recent project? What has been your greatest achievement? Why is (topic) important to you? What did you learn from that experience?	To introduce topics — broad focus. To gain an insight of beyond the CV. Invites the candidate to 'open up' using their own words. To discover the candidate's attitudes.
Depth	Tell me a bit more about the project? What exactly was your role in the project? What did you do then? How did you measure your success?	Signals that you want the candidate to give more information. To test for detail or depth. To focus on the candidate's actual role, activity, competence and performance.
Summarising or rephrasing	So, You told me that [...] have I understood that correctly?	Reflect the candidate's words back to them for confirmation. This gives the candidate an invitation for further comment.
Provocative (challenging or probing)	What happens if the pilot project is not a success? What happens if your project sponsor leaves? So, what you are saying is that the project failed?	To test for a deeper understanding of the subject. Requires thinking. Provocation to see how the candidate reacts to, or corrects, the perception.

Know what kind of answer to expect and be prepared for alternatives. In an assessment, if you've asked a candidate, say, about project management, you need to know how to understand their answer. Hence, designing questions includes notes of what a good answer consists of. Be aware that the candidate might offer answers that you haven't thought of; as the assessor, you also need to keep an open mind to accept answers beyond your knowledge.

For example, using the project management example, a candidate might offer a response saying, *"I use the agile systems approach to project management ..."*. If your project management expertise does not include agile systems, then a follow up question in the form of *"Tell me more about agile systems ..."* is a good way of assessing the candidate's ability to communicate, and indeed might be something extra that the candidate could bring to your organisation. (See also the section on 'hooks' in 11.5.4.)

The output from the design phase is a question plan, and agenda, broadly following s a sequence such as:

Warm-up questions
Design a few simple and safe questions (probably closed questions with short answers) to settle a candidate into the assessment.

Theme based questions,

- Competency seeking questions — to discover the candidate's talents and suitability.

- Follow-up questions — To discover if the candidate has substantial experience and the depth of that experience.

- Challenge questions — to place an obstacle in the answer thus forcing the candidate to work around it.

- Summarising questions

Knowledge questions

Design knowledge seeking questions to discover what the candidate knows.

- Follow-up questions — To discover the depth of candidate's knowledge.

- Provocative questions — to place a complication or unusual circumstance to ascertain if the candidate can solve the problem.

- Summarising questions

Remember to assign an approximate time for each questioning theme.

Worked Example:

In this questioning sequence, the objective is to discover the candidate's competence in planning and organising.

Interviewer: *"Tell me about one of **your** recent projects"*
Candidate: *"It was about marketing a new product to..."*

Interviewer: *"What was **your** role in the project?"*
Candidate: *"**My** role was to work with the design agency to..."*

Interviewer: *"What exactly did **you** have to do?"*
Candidate: *"..."*

Interviewer: *"Were **you** successful?"*
Candidate: *"..."*

Interviewer: *"What might **you** do differently next time?"*
Candidate: *"..."*

The purpose of any question is to seek a response from the candidate that provides information and evidence that you can match to a competence.

Don't 'think' of questions
— design them.

8.3 The toolkit for ability tests

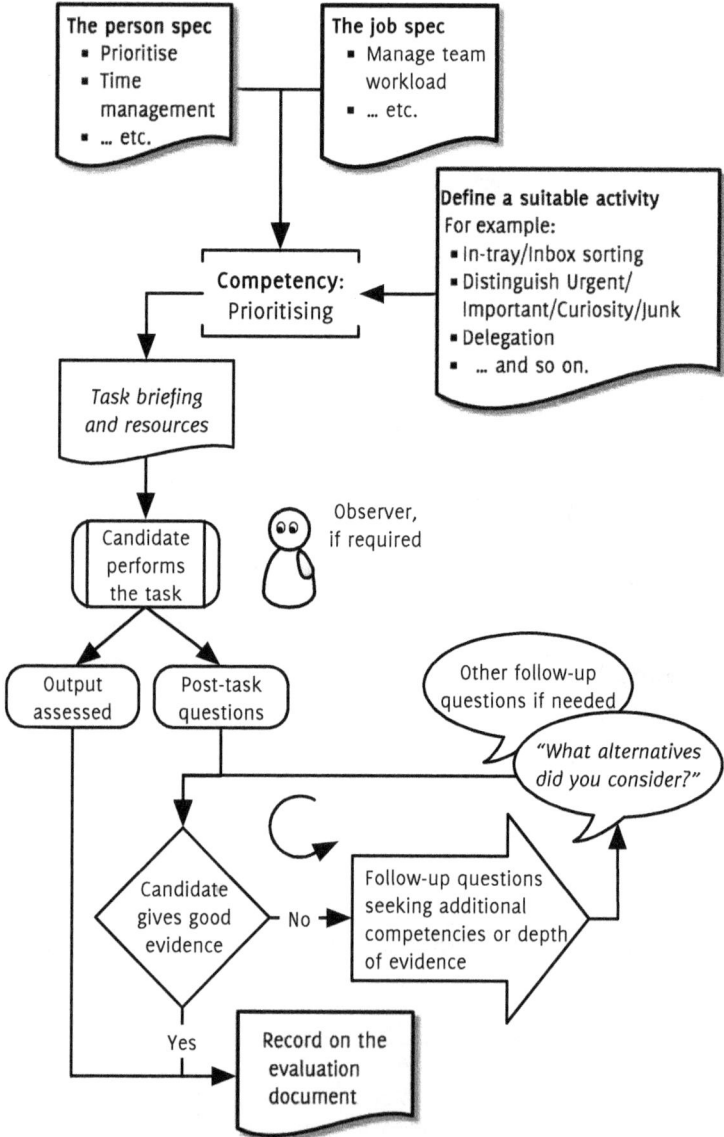

The person spec
- Prioritise
- Time management
- ... etc.

The job spec
- Manage team workload
- ... etc.

Define a suitable activity
For example:
- In-tray/Inbox sorting
- Distinguish Urgent/ Important/Curiosity/Junk
- Delegation
- ... and so on.

Competency: Prioritising

Task briefing and resources

Candidate performs the task

Observer, if required

Output assessed

Post-task questions

Other follow-up questions if needed

"What alternatives did you consider?"

Candidate gives good evidence

No →

Follow-up questions seeking additional competencies or depth of evidence

Yes

Record on the evaluation document

Figure 9 — Designing activities

8.3.1 The role of ability tests

An ability test is a practical activity so you can assess the candidate's capability to perform a prescribed activity. The activity can range from manual handling to intellectual application.

If you decide to use an ability test, your role as project leader is to design and test an activity that enables a candidate to display their behaviours, skills, or knowledge, so that you can observe and record their capabilities.

8.3.2 Design goals for ability tests

The breadth of ability tests is large; at one extreme, an ability test can be a task, for example performing some maintenance or assembly such as fitting an automotive part, or for a hair stylist, cutting someone's hair. At the other extreme, it could be a case study that the candidate studies and analyses, and then presents a strategy. Some ability tests might be standard or required for your industry sector.

The design goals for ability tests includes:

Link ability tests to the role specifications
An activity must be relevant to the role; there should be a clear linkage between the role specifications and the activity, so that the candidate can display the competencies you are assessing.

Irrelevant activities are a waste of time and little value beyond the curiosity of the assessor. There is also a danger that the candidate leaves the assessment and wonders what it was all about, then tells others of the negative experience (brand damage).

Clarity of the task
To get the best out of the candidates, the task you give them must clear in what you want them to do. There are three parts to clarity:

1) The briefing — clear and unambiguous statements about what is to be achieved. One method of doing this is to use directive language, for example:

"Your task is to ...".
"We want you to ..."
"Your job is to ..."

To ascertain that the candidate has understood the task, you can ask the candidate to repeat it back to you. This is especially useful in spoken instructions, and if you observe the candidate making notes, this is a small but useful indicator of being organised.

2) The resources — the provision of resources, for example tools and materials. (Note: in some crafts and professions, people always use their own tools. For example, hairdressers rarely share their scissors.) If candidates are required to bring their own tools, highlight this fact in the invitation. (Although, a back up is always a good idea.)

3) The deliverable — clarity of what the candidate is to produce or have achieved by the end of the allocated time.
Examples:

"An assembled widget ready for inspection by the assessor."
"A ten-minute presentation with a preferred strategy from the case study."

If there are multiple tasks, make it clear whether the candidate must do them in a fixed order or in any order; to do them at their own pace (spending more or less time with each task) or at a fixed pace.

Know what a suitable deliverable is, and be prepared for alternatives
For activities where the deliverable involves choices or creativity, you might not get the result you predicted. Nevertheless, if the deliverable satisfies the criteria in the job and person specifications, the activity has enabled the candidate to display the competencies and you should score the result appropriately.

Table 7 — A toolkit of ability tests

Type of activity	Examples	When to use
Practical, Trade tests	An activity, often timed and observed, to establish if the applicant can do something specific. Typical tests include: equipment maintenance, preparing a classic cocktail drink, typing accurately at certain rate, writing a segment of computer code.	To assess the skill and level of skill. To assess accuracy, completeness, or safety.
Logic or procedural	Step-by-step assembly. Building a model or machine from its component parts. Project organisation	Use where the role involves working through process or complex problem solving situations.
Verbal Reasoning	Creating summaries and précis. Drafting a response to a customer complaint. Comprehension of written information or instructions	Use where there is a need to understand the written word (literacy).
Numerical Reasoning	Creating a spreadsheet from supplied data. Estimation skills. Application of statistical, financial, or budgetary, figures.	Use where there is a need to understand the numerical information (numeracy). Use for a role that involves working with data/calculations.
Spatial awareness	A craft activity, such as assembling an intricate object, drawing or sketching. Moving apparatus.	Use in situations where the role involves work with intricate parts, physical manoeuvres, or coordinated lifting and handling within a team.

8.3.3   The design output — Activity plan and briefing

At the end of the design phase, an activity has the appearance of a small project (which it is) and contains:

- A briefing for the assessors and observers.

- A briefing for the candidate (including pre-briefing if they are to bring their own tools). This includes a safety briefing relevant to the place where the task takes place.

- A resource list.

- Restrictions, for example limitations arising from health and safety.

- Space and place requirements.

- Time allocations.

8.4   The toolkit for interviews

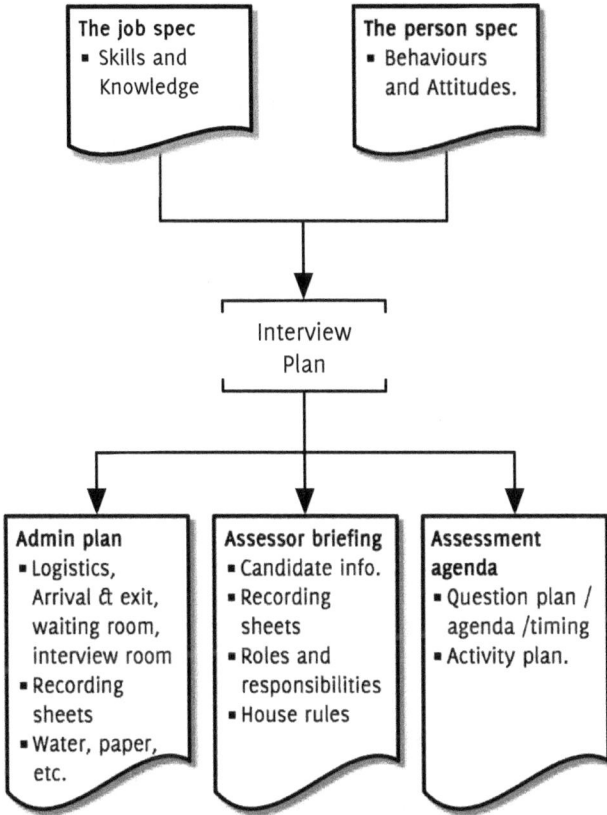

```
┌──────────────────┐      ┌──────────────────┐
│ The job spec     │      │ The person spec  │
│ ▪ Skills and     │      │ ▪ Behaviours     │
│   Knowledge      │      │   and Attitudes. │
└──────────────────┘      └──────────────────┘
```

Interview Plan

```
┌──────────────────┐  ┌──────────────────┐  ┌──────────────────┐
│ Admin plan       │  │ Assessor briefing│  │ Assessment       │
│ ▪ Logistics,     │  │ ▪ Candidate info.│  │ agenda           │
│   Arrival & exit,│  │ ▪ Recording      │  │ ▪ Question plan /│
│   waiting room,  │  │   sheets         │  │   agenda /timing │
│   interview room │  │ ▪ Roles and      │  │ ▪ Activity plan. │
│ ▪ Recording      │  │   responsibilities│ │                  │
│   sheets         │  │ ▪ House rules    │  │                  │
│ ▪ Water, paper,  │  │                  │  │                  │
│   etc.           │  │                  │  │                  │
└──────────────────┘  └──────────────────┘  └──────────────────┘
```

Figure 10 — Toolkit for interviews

8.4.1   The purpose of an interview

The purpose of an interview is to assess the candidate's suitability for the role. The advantage of an interview is that you gain first-hand accounts of their experience and direct observations of the candidate performing an activity. You can quiz the candidate for extra detail, see how well they meet the specifications, and ascertain their behaviours and attitudes. The assessment can be a single interview with one or more assessors, or a series of interviews each with one or more assessors.

You can assume a good candidate has prepared for their interview; you need to be equally well prepared. You cannot 'wing-it' because you think you'll know a competence when you see it; that is simply hoping for a good answer rather than designing for a best outcome.

There is a finite amount of time you can spend in an interview, which in turn restricts how much evidence can be gathered for each criterion. The interview needs to be effective: an effective interview requires planning and design.

In designing the assessment interview the aim is to engage the candidate, seeking corroborative evidence of competence. It is important not to miss key points for the candidate record and the to spot the opportunity to generate related, supplementary questions.

This requires a single interviewer to multi-task by:

- Asking questions.
- Actively listening to the answers.
- Observing the candidate's behaviour.
- Generate and ask supplementary questions.
- Record the notes.

... all without completely sacrificing eye contact! It is recommended that help and support is built-in at the design stage. For example: a note-taker or a second interviewer to ask questions, observers, and assessors.

8.4.2   Design goals for an interview

Generally, an interview involves asking questions, listening to the answers, keeping the candidate on-track, and recording the evidence matching the specifications. Remember to treat the candidate as a customer — design the their experience so that they become ambassadors and speak well of you afterwards (even if they don't get the job).

In a one-hour interview, there is time for about five themes of enquiry.

The specific goals for designing an interview include:

1) Create an interviewing environment

There are three main aspects to designing an interview:

i) The place and space — this is where the interview is to be held. It includes the room, the furniture, decorations*, light, heat, whiteboards, projector and screen.

> (*) Decorations include company posters, flipcharts, and litter such as leftover documents or training notes. These might be invisible to you because of your familiarity with the material; to a candidate it is a cause of distraction. Examine (preferably remove) these to be certain that no sensitive information is being displayed, so whatever is visible displays a positive image of your organisation.

ii) The people Involved — the assessor team (including observers) and those who might pop into the room during the interview; the action is to create a briefing so that everyone knows their roles.

iii) The content of the interview — the questions and answers.

2) Link the interview to the vacancy

A useful way for the chairman of the interview to start is to briefly remind everyone what they are there for; so a short prepared set-piece welcoming the candidate, then reminding the candidate and the interviewers what job is being applied for. (There is an example in chapter 10.5.) This synchronising statement avoids a potentially embarrassing moment when part way through an interview for, say, a photocopier service technician, the candidate suddenly thanks you for an interesting question, and asks, *"but what is the connection with gas fitting vacancy I applied for?"*

3) Link interview to the specifications

Using the question plan from 8.2 provides the linkage to job and person specifications.

4) Choose the type of interview appropriate to the competency

There are four common types of interview. Each serves a different purpose and with care in the selection of the questions, all types can be incorporated into a single interview session. These are summarised in Table 8.

Table 8 — A toolkit of interview approaches

Type of assessment	Examples	When to use
Competency based interview	A typical start to a competency-based question is: *"Tell me about a situation when ..."*	To test for the candidate's behaviours and attitudes based on recollections from real life experiences in their career. The advantage of this approach is that the candidate's evidence is based on facts from experience. You might need multiple questions to probe the evidence.
Intellectual Application based interview	A typical approach is: Describe a situation; give the candidate a specific role in that situation, a complication, and an objective. (See Note 1 following.)	To test the intellect of the candidate and often involves problem solving, typically by using knowledge in one context and applying it in another.
Knowledge based interview	For example, *"Tell me which colour wire goes to which terminal on a UK 13amp domestic plug?"* To probe for deep knowledge, ask a provocative question, for example, *"what would happen if the green/yellow wire and the brown wire were swapped?"*	To discover what the candidates know. Their knowledge might not be supported by experiences; it might be the result of education, private learning, or personal research. The purpose of this is to ascertain whether the candidate has relevant knowledge. (See Note 2 following.)

Type of assessment	Examples	When to use
Behavioural based interview	Interview questions can provide credible examples of teamwork, leading and motivating a team or project. A typical question might be *"Tell me about what you learnt from a situation when you dealt with success/failure, challenges/conflict ..."* The candidate's response might include evidence of persistence and endeavour, taking accountability, motivating self and others. What work would the candidate never undertake?	Observation of candidates in a group activity or simulation can provide direct evidence of behaviours, for example, does a candidate take a proactive, dominant role in a group discussion or do they sit back and listen? Do they build on the ideas of others, giving credit where it is due or do they dampen enthusiasm and kill ideas without consideration?

Note 1

An example of the Situation, Role, Complication and Objective format is something like this: "I'd like you to imagine that you are the leader (the role) of a youth club (the situation). The club has twenty members and all have varying levels of physical disability (the complication). They would like to go on a vacation (the objective). How would you set about this challenge?"

Additionally, the ability to make decisions can be tested: once the candidate has developed a solution, take the candidate back to the beginning and ask them to develop a different solution. At the end of this theme, the candidate has delivered two equally good solutions. Requiring the candidate to choose one is a test of their reasoning and decision-making capability.

Note 2

Be aware that knowledge varies along a scale. Shallow knowledge is simply recall without necessarily the understanding (think of television quiz shows). Deep knowledge is required to apply that knowledge to an unusual situation.

8.4.3   The design output — Interview plan and briefing

The output from designing an interview is a set of requirements and briefing documents.

The requirements include:

- Requirements for the interview room
- Requirements for the resources and materials
- Requirements of the assessor team (putting the candidate at ease, breaks for note taking and refreshments, time to reflect and recuperate).

The briefings include:

- Roles and responsibilities of every person involved in the interview.
- An interview plan with the agenda and timings.

> Your preparation directly impacts the candidate's performance

8.5 The toolkit for group assessments

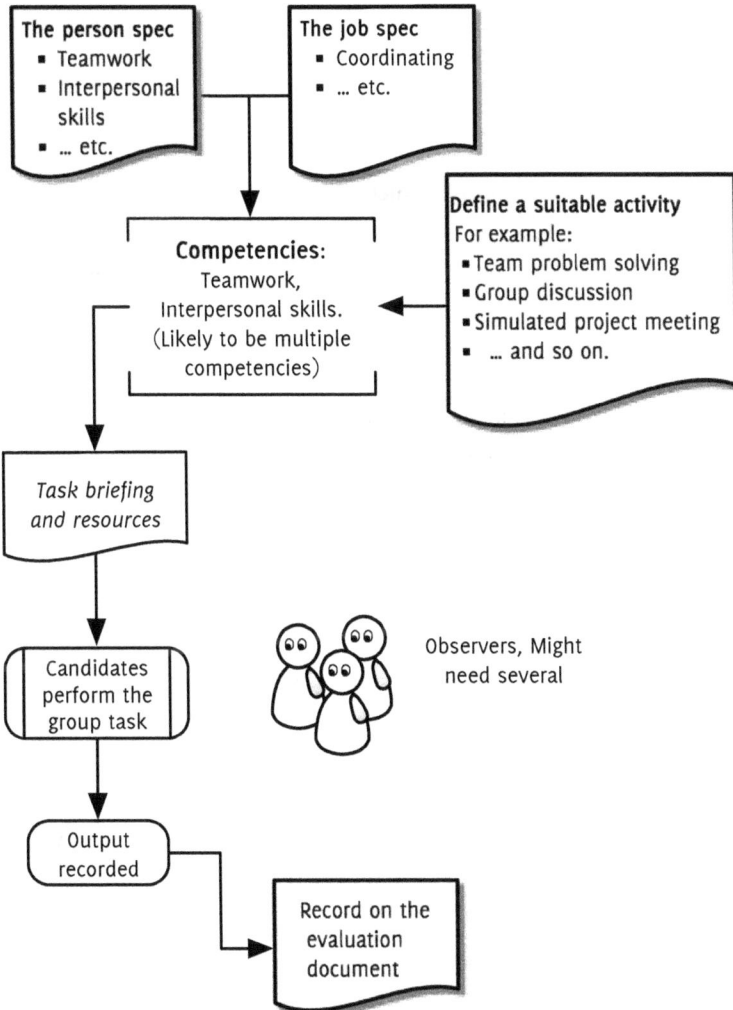

The person spec
- Teamwork
- Interpersonal skills
- ... etc.

The job spec
- Coordinating
- ... etc.

Competencies:
Teamwork,
Interpersonal skills.
(Likely to be multiple competencies)

Define a suitable activity
For example:
- Team problem solving
- Group discussion
- Simulated project meeting
- ... and so on.

Task briefing and resources

Candidates perform the group task

Observers, Might need several

Output recorded

Record on the evaluation document

Figure 11 — Design of group assessments

8.5.1 The role of group assessments

A group assessment enables you to observe several candidates at the same time. Remember that the candidates are in competition with each other and the opportunity for a devious candidate to game the situation is ever present, as is the possibility for dysfunctional behaviour to emerge.

Although each candidate performs their role or task within a group, remember that you are assessing each candidate as an individual.

8.5.2 Design goals for group assessments

The design factors for group activities are for the most part similar to those for individual activities. However, group dynamics complicates the design and observation of the candidates.

1) Link ability tests to the specifications

The group activity should be relevant to the specifications. It is likely that a teamwork competency drives the group activity. If so, it is important to define what kind of behaviour is required and desired for the particular type of team.

> Note:
>> There are many different types of team, for example, a team that shares similar expertise and each member is interchangeable. A different type of team is formed from those with dissimilar expertise contribute specific elements to the whole activity. Other titles in the Leadership Library address this topic.

2) Clarity of the task

In a group context, each member is likely to understand a briefing a little differently. The task needs to be clear, and an early observation might be to watch the group test their own understanding of the objective.

3) Equal opportunity to contribute

In a group, each candidate must have a fair opportunity to contribute and observed displaying their competencies and behaviours within the group. This does make the role of observers more demanding; they must keep track of those who quietly contribute to the group, and those who noisily contribute little.

Table 9 — A toolkit of for group activities

Type of activity	Examples	When to use
A facilitated group discussion	A discussion group led by a competent chairman; supported by observers. Topics can be current affairs or specific industry news. For example: *"What has been happening in the news that affects mental health nursing?"*	To assess the candidates awareness of the larger picture in which organisation operates. To assess, team skills such as building on others' contributions.
A problem to be solved	An Intellectual Application problem (using the Situation, Role, Complications, Goal format). A large format puzzle, for example the assembly of interconnected objects following a schematic. Analysis of some case-study information, followed by a group presentation.	To assess problem solving skills in a team working context. For example, suggesting and assigning/taking roles; summarising, moving things forward; leadership, involving others; process and coordination To assess clarity of giving feedback as a group.
A competition	Two teams are given an identical task but are aware that another team is doing the same. (See note below)	To assess the 'winner' desire in a candidate. To assess whether the teams can work out that cooperation gives a better outcome.

Note:
Be very careful of using a competition unless it is vital to the job role. Competitions can result in dysfunctional behaviour such as sabotage. Likewise, be aware that familiar stereotypes can direct the candidate to falsify their behaviour. For example, the aggressive target-driven sales role works in some cases, but in others, relationship building and consultative behaviour are the required characteristics.

8.5.3   The design output — Activity plan and briefing

The output from designing an interview is a set of requirements and briefing documents.

The requirements include:

- The place and space requirements for the group activity. In some circumstances this might be large floor area.

- Requirements for the resources and materials. (Includes Personal Protection Equipment for industrial areas.)

The briefings include:

- The description of the activity for the candidates.

- A description of the activity for the assessors and observers, including:

  - Roles and responsibilities of the assessors/observers, and

  - What behaviours and competencies are being sought?

- Agenda and timings.

- In an industrial environment health and safety is paramount so also include a safety briefing.

8.6 The toolkit for presentations in assessment

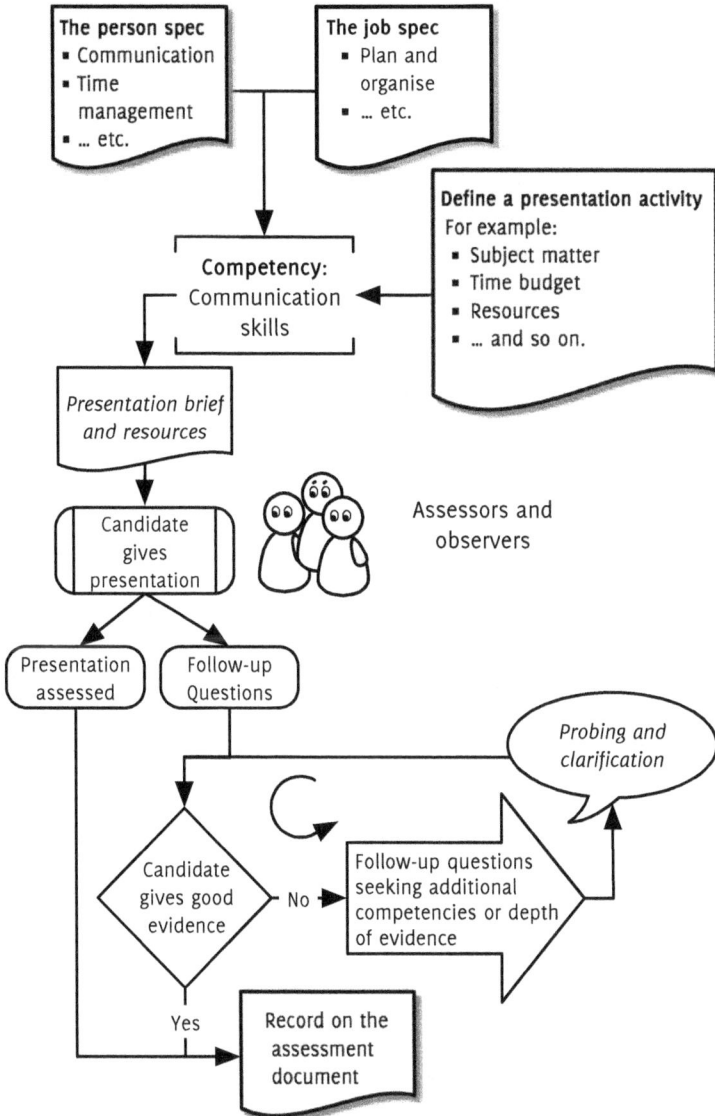

Figure 12 — Design of presentation activities

8.6.1 The role of presentation assessments

Asking a candidate to deliver a presentation enables the assessors to observe a candidate's communication and influencing skills. In leadership roles, the ability to give convincing presentations is often an essential attribute in the person specification.

A presentation can demonstrate the same capabilities as an interview: competency, knowledge, and intellect. And hence need similar planning to give clarity on the objective and how it is assessed. When using presentations as a method of assessment ensure that the assessment team and the candidate's are clear on what is being observed and assessed.

8.6.2 Design goals for presentation assessments

The two main dimensions of assessing a candidate's abilities using a presentation are:

Presentation delivery
The impact of a presentation is a consequence of how it is delivered. These soft skills can be more important than the content.
In assessing presentation delivery, you are looking for how well the candidate engaged their audience, (that is, you and the assessor team). Engagement is the sum of presentation structure, their pacing and rhythm, tone and clarity of voice, eye contact and physical gestures.

Content
The basic choices for subject matter are either to let the candidate choose their own topic, or to give all candidates the same topic (or topic theme if is the result of a case study). Giving the candidate a free choice is likely to produce some interesting topics and associated forms of delivery. A fixed choice might make it easier to assess on a like-for-like basis.

In technical interviews, you might ask a candidate to present an explanation of how something works. Everyday technical examples might be: how does a fluorescent light work; at graduate level, explain how Ethernet works in a local area network.

The toolkit for presentations in assessments includes:

1) Link the presentation assessment to the specifications
The ability to plan, prepare, and deliver a presentation should already be in the job specifications, together with the circumstance and type of audience.

2) Clarity of presentation topic
For fair assessments, you must make it clear to the candidate what is expected, what are the freedoms and the restrictions.

The presentation brief should be included in the invitation. In an assessment centre approach, give all candidates the same briefing notes and resources.

3) Role and behaviour of the assessors
The behaviour of the assessor panel can affect the performance of the candidate. Behaviours such as head-down taking notes, loosing eye contact, and similar convey a lack of interest. Hence, it is important that the panel are briefed on what is expected of them throughout the delivery of the presentation. This briefing includes: who is present, their roles, and the protocol or etiquette for asking questions of the candidate.

4) Resources and visual aids
These days, one automatically makes a link between a presentation and a computer with a projector; however it is a poor assumption. The range of what a presentation might be is much larger. It can be a stand-up talk without visual aids of any kind. It can be a stand-up talk with props and flipcharts; they can be desk-based presentations using a display portfolio, right though to multi-media extravaganzas.
Computers and the like, obey Murphy's Law — *if it can go wrong, it will*. In planning the resources, ensure there are backups. And vitally, always check for compatibility. There are benefits in asking candidate to bring their own laptop or tablet together with a briefing on what and how they can connect to the projector.

5) Know what a suitable presentation is, and be prepared for surprise alternatives

Keep in mind that you might disagree with the candidate's specific content and this could bias your assessment of the their performance. To ensure fairness, the assessment criteria should focus on elements such as: structure, logical progression, and reaching a conclusion (not necessarily the conclusion itself). In knowledge based presentations you might be looking for specific content.

6) Assessment criteria

To assess a candidate's presentation, consider these criteria:

- Audience engagement,
- Structure of the material,
- Clarity of points made,
- Handling of questions
- Planning and preparation,
- Time management,
- Pace, tone,
- Supporting gestures.

Remember, a candidate's presentation might include material with which you disagree, perhaps on technical merit, perhaps it conflicts with your experiences, or more dangerously, it clashes with your beliefs. The way out of this problem is to stick to what is being assessed. Unless you are looking for specific material to be conveyed (set-subject presentations) then you are assessing the candidate's ability to present effectively.

Table 10 — A toolkit of interview approaches

Format of presentation	Examples	When to use
Candidate's choice of topic	A ten-minute presentation on (for example) any subject of the candidate's choice (see note below).	Use when you want to demonstrate presentation skills; where the subject matter is not critical to the role.
Fixed topic	A ten-minute presentation on current developments in energy generation.	Use when you want the candidate to demonstrate their knowledge and the ability to communicate it to others.

Note — An Example: In one interview an industrial process engineer choose *The superstitions concerning women on ships* for her topic. The interview panel learnt a great deal from an engaging presentation, and were able to deduce and assess her planning and researching skills, and observe how she presented her topic.

8.6.3 The Design output — for presentations

Including a presentation as an assessment activity requires considerable design and preparation. Among the design outputs are requirements and briefings:

The requirements include:

- The place and space requirements for a presentation.

- Requirements for the resources and materials — including IT equipment (laptop, screen) flipchart easel/pens/paper, and so on.

- Briefings for:

  - The specification of the presentation for the candidate.

  - The role, responsibilities, and behaviours of the assessors.

- Assessment schema and associated paperwork for use in the evaluation.

8.7 Personality questionnaires

An ability or trade test provides a result or a score. By contrast, a personality questionnaire reflects an individual's personal preferences.

Personality questionnaires are not an objective assessment of a person's capability or a predictor of success in a role. They are not recommended for use in recruitment and selection programmes.

A preference or interest level indicated by a personality questionnaire might mean that the candidate has acquired knowledge or gained practical skill in that area yet it does not necessarily mean that they are any good at it. For example, a candidate who prefers detail might also be good at working with the detail. Conversely it does not mean that the same candidate cannot see the 'big picture' when they need to work at that level, only that they prefer the detail.

If used, caution must be exercised in the weighting and value given to this type of questionnaire in your overall assessment. Ideally, personality questionnaires should only be used to confirm the decisions that would otherwise be made from more objective and deterministic assessments.

Personality questionnaires are unreliable predictors of success in a role.

9   The toolkit for evaluation

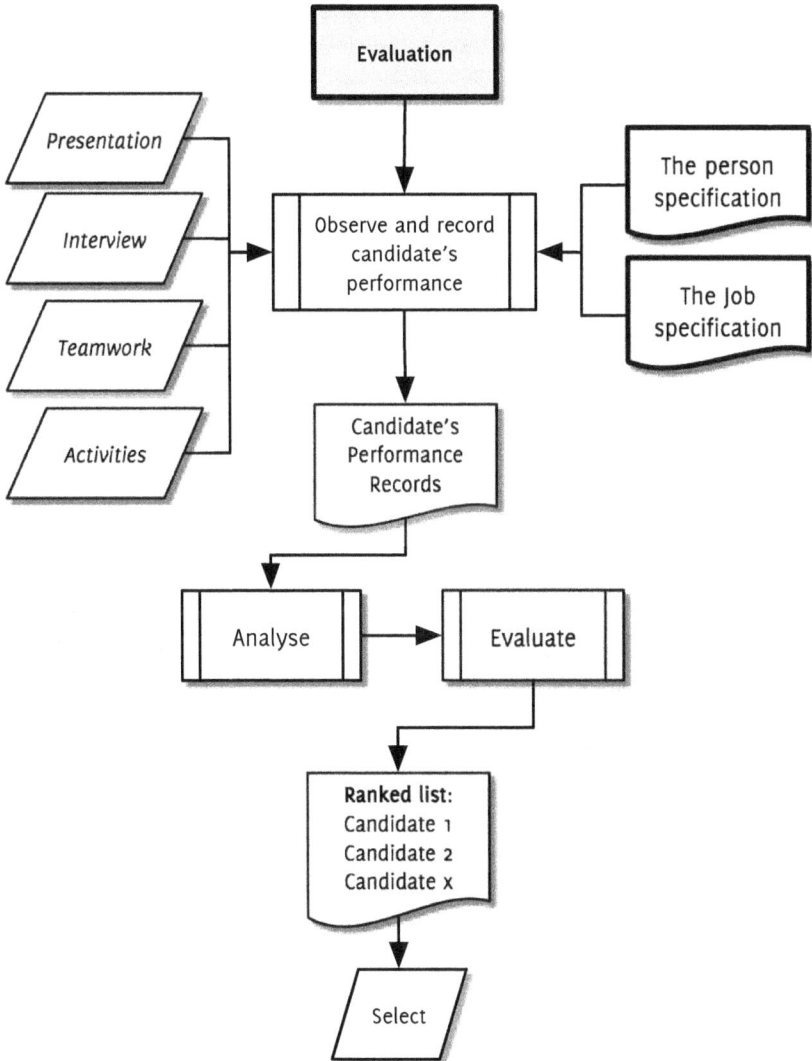

Figure 13 — Assessment and evaluation

9.1 The purpose of evaluation

The purpose of evaluation is to review the outcome of the assessments and produce a ranked list from which you are able to select the best available candidate for the role and for your organisation. Evaluation is the critical point at which you compare and contrast all the information and assessment evidence provided by each candidate against the essential and desirable criteria for the role.

9.2 Evaluation principles

Evaluation criteria should be:

- Based on and aligned with the job and person specifications.

- Agreed between the project leader and the project owner.
  This avoids the risk of an excellent method recruiting the wrong person.

- Straightforward to administer. This means:

  - Design each evaluation criterion in the simplest and most direct way possible.
    (Simplest means the least complex; it does not mean simplistic.)

  - Use plain English in recording sheets.

  - If you are using a spreadsheet to record and rank scores, keep the functions and arithmetic simple. (Spreadsheets can be error-prone in the hands of the unskilled.)

- Fair and consistent for all candidates (internal and external).

- Free from selection biases.

9.3 Evaluation design

9.3.1 Core elements of evaluation design

The three core elements of designing evaluation into an assessment activity are:

- For each activity, define the critical-few evaluation criteria. If you define too many, the resulting score tends follows the mathematical phenomenon known as the central limit theorem in which the overall score becomes the average of all scores which then leaves you with little to differentiate among the candidates.

- For each criterion define the **range** of possible scores; and

- For each criterion assign a **weighting** factor that represents how important it is.

9.3.2 Range

Range is the granularity of the score that can be given by an assessor. The selection of range depends on the complexity or depth of the criterion. Common ranges of scores are:

A two-level range

A two-level range is characterised by the answer to a closed question: *Does the candidate...?* The range of possible assessments is therefore Yes or No. It is best used for simple tick-list assessments, for example:

- Does the candidate hold a current driving license?

- Does the candidate hold the xyz qualification?

In a spreadsheet code 'yes' as the number 1, and 'no' as the number 0 (zero) — this is important when evaluation arithmetic is calculated.

> Note:
> The reason to use numbers scores is that spreadsheets cannot (should not) multiply a text field (say, the word 'yes') by a number — you'll end up with the #VALUE! error.

A three-level range

A three-level range is useful where the assessment activity is expected to produce some granular variation in the assessment. A typical form of a three-level assessment is:

- The candidate gave no evidence matching the criterion (score = 0)
- The candidate gave evidence to meet the criterion (score = 1)
- The candidate gave evidence that exceeds the criterion (score = 2).

Alternatively, classify as Low/Medium/High. (Scoring 0, 1, 2, respectively.)

A four level range

A four-level range gives some extra granularity to differentiate the candidates. In this case the discrete scoring is:

- The candidate did not give evidence for the criterion (score = 0)
- The candidate gave some evidence and partially demonstrated competence for the criterion. (score = 1)
- The candidate gave sufficient evidence to fully meet the competences for the criterion. (score = 2)
- The candidate gave evidence which exceeds the competencies for the criterion (score = 3)

Higher-level ranges

Higher-level ranges are useful where finer distinctions are required. A zero to five (six-level range) or a zero to ten (eleven-level range) is workable. Take care that wide range also follows the central limit theorem and the scores tend to cluster around the average ultimately leaving you with no distinguishing factors among the candidates.

9.3.3 Weighting

A weighting factor is a number that represents how important a criterion is. Each criterion needs an associated weighting factor.

In evaluation, the score given to the criterion is multiplied by the weighting factor to produce a weighted score.

$$C_1 \times W_1 = \text{Weighted Score for Criterion 1.}$$

Weighting factors are small numbers. The basic weighting factor is 1. A criterion that is somewhat more important is about 1.2 to 1.5 so that when multiplied by the criterion score it boosts the weighted score. A weighting factor beyond $\times 2$ would exaggerate that criterion and overwhelm the weighted scores from other criteria; it suggests that the original list of essential criteria is unsound.

9.4   Designing an evaluation grid

In readiness for the moment after all candidates have been assessed, create a recording sheet to hold the criterion range, the weighting factors, and the underlying arithmetic to calculate the candidates' weighted scores.

An example is shown in Table 11 below. In this example, three assessment activities are shown: The presentation activity has three criteria, (C_1, C_2, C_3); all three are scored from zero to five. The weighting factors are different for each criterion; in this example, C_3 has the highest weighting of 1.8.

The evaluation grid assists your objective evaluation of each candidate. While the overall candidate-weighted calculations produces a ranked list, an additional benefit is that the grid highlights where the candidates met or exceeded the criteria.

9.5   Design notes

A single activity might be assessed against three criteria: C_1, C_2, and C_3. Each criterion can have a different range; there is no requirement that each criterion should have an identical range.

You may want to consider how evidence of additional, skills, knowledge, or experience can be calibrated and evaluated to differentiate the candidates in your final analysis.

Table 11 — Example of an evaluation grid

Activity	Presentation			Group Discussion					Business Case			
Criteria	C_1	C_2	C_3	C_1	C_2	C_3	C_4	C_5	C_1	C_2	C_3	C_4
Range (0-to-max.)	5	5	5	3	3	3	3	3	5	5	5	3
Weighting factor	1.0	1.2	1.8	1.2	1	1	1.2	1.2	1	2	2	1
Maximum Possible Score	20			16.8					18			
Candidate's assessed Score	4	3	5	3	3	1	0	2	3	3	2	1
Candidate's Weighted Score	16.6			9					14			

The creation of an evaluation grid provides you with an at-a-glance numerical summary for the overall performance of all the candidates, which guides you to your initial ranked list.

Range and weighting help to differentiate your candidates.

10 Leading the assessor team

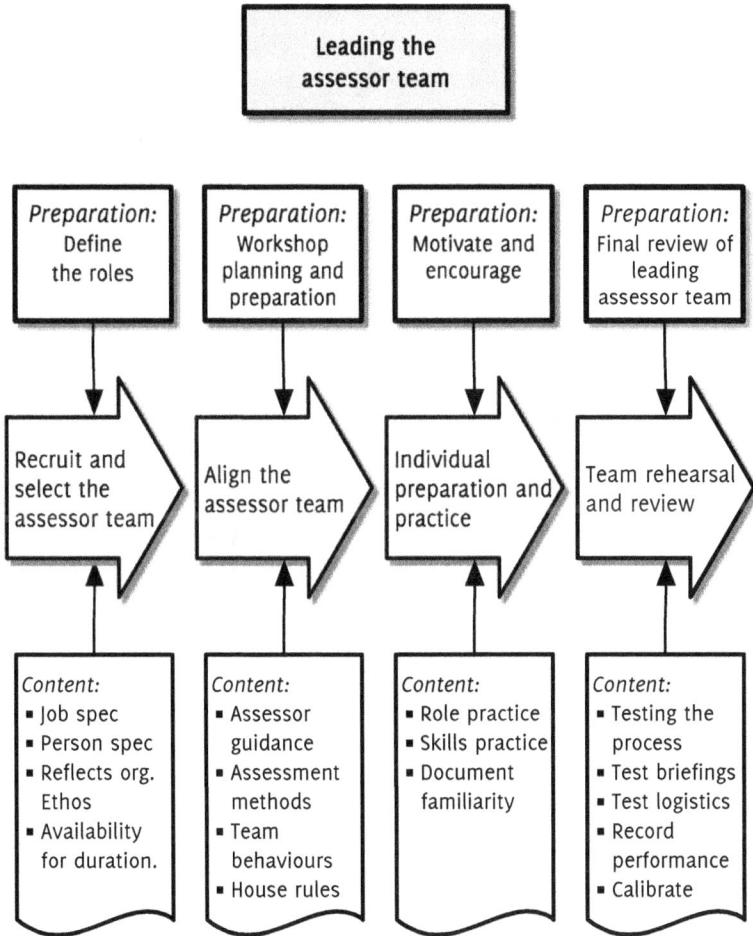

Leading the assessor team

| *Preparation:* Define the roles | *Preparation:* Workshop planning and preparation | *Preparation:* Motivate and encourage | *Preparation:* Final review of leading assessor team |

| Recruit and select the assessor team | Align the assessor team | Individual preparation and practice | Team rehearsal and review |

| *Content:*
 • Job spec
 • Person spec
 • Reflects org. Ethos
 • Availability for duration. | *Content:*
 • Assessor guidance
 • Assessment methods
 • Team behaviours
 • House rules | *Content:*
 • Role practice
 • Skills practice
 • Document familiarity | *Content:*
 • Testing the process
 • Test briefings
 • Test logistics
 • Record performance
 • Calibrate |

Figure 14 — Leading the assessor team

10.1 The assessor team is the company

From the candidate's perspective, the assessors represent their potential employer. If the assessors are disorganised, the employer is disorganised; if the assessors don't work as one team, the employer is not a team player. It is your job as the project leader to prepare the assessment team so that you select the best candidate and leave the unselected candidates with a positive view of your company.

Leading the Assessment team is an important role in recruitment and selection project so your team performs an effective, fair, and equitable assessment.

The assessment team follows a development life cycle that can be summarised as:

- Select the assessors, then...

- Align the team so they understand the project objective, so that each assessor knows their role and responsibilities within the project.

- Rehearse and calibrate the activities and observations so each candidate is assessed to the same standard.

- Undertake the assessments, observe, record, compare, and evaluate.

- Participation in reviews and selection.

- Participation in the end of project review and project closure.

The assessment team look to you for guidance and support in doing their part.

10.2 Selecting the assessor team

Choosing an assessor team is a mini recruitment and selection project in its own right; you can use similar approaches to select assessor team members. A good place to start is a job and person specification.

Table 12 — Job/role and person specifications for assessors

The role	The person
• To observe and record candidate performance [P] • Availability for the duration of the project. [E] • Present a professional appearance to the team and the candidates. [E] • Display the organisation's ethos and values at all times. [E] • Knowledge and experience of the assessment process and plan. [E] • Relevant qualifications or subject matter expertise (where required) [E] • Remain objective and impartial [E] • Plus any others to suit your project's needs. [E or D as required]	• Willing and able, and motivated to contribute to all aspects of the project (planning and preparation through to debrief and project closure) [E] • Assessing skills, behaviours and presence [E] • Assessment experience [E] • Experience of questioning techniques, listening (and use of silence), observing, and recording. [E] • Communication skills. [E] • Can takes a holistic approach to the assessment [E] • Able to create developmental feedback [E] • Plus any others to suit your project's needs. [E or D as required]

Key: P – Purpose, E – Essential, D – Desirable
Note: you might need to train the team in assessment skills.

You can be, and in some cases must be, discerning in the selection of the assessment team. You might find that choice of available assessors includes people from operations, line management, HR or external assessors. The tricky part is to select those who can provide a balanced, objective assessment of the candidates. You might need considerable diplomacy when creating an effective assessor team.

Some attributes for selecting your assessor team are summarised in Table 13:

Table 13 — Some attributes for selecting assessors

Appoint	Avoid appointing
• Based on suitability, current qualification and experience • Open-minded individuals, who can suspend their judgement until the evaluation stage • Individuals whose business and personal objectives align. For example individuals seeking to develop their assessor capability • Someone who is independent of the role	• The usual suspects simply because they are available and they always do the assessing • Purely on rank or seniority — this is not a guarantee of effective assessment • 'Prima Donnas' with egos to massage or anyone who 'grandstands' • Anyone that might overrule, influence, or correct the candidates • Judgementalists who are 'always right'

An effective assessor team enables your project to make progress.

10.3 Creating the assessor team

10.3.1 Aligning the team

Once your assessor team has been recruited into your project, the first job is to align them into a cohesive team. A cohesive assessor team acts as one entity with one approach and one voice. A workshop is a good way to create this alignment.

An agenda for such a workshop might flow as follows:

- Introductory briefing
    - Aim of the project (give each member a copy of the PID).
    - Theory and methods to select the best person for the job.
    - Ethos of getting the best from the candidates.
    - Project objectives — what the organisation is trying to achieve.

- Introductions — having heard the briefing, what does each team member consider their role to be?

  - You should lead by example:
    "Good morning, my name is Jayne; my role is to be an operational assessor for the technology aspects of the assessments."

    Note: This is an engagement method to form a new team.

  - Why do they want to be a member of the assessment team? This draws out the alignment of their personal and business objectives. It is important to you in understanding their motivation and commitment to the assessor role and the project objectives.

- Details then include, for example:

  - A review and clarity of the job and person specifications

  - The outline plan.

  - The assessment approach and toolkit

  - House rules for the assessors. (See note.)

  - Expected behaviours of the team

  - ... and so on... so that each assessor has a clear understanding of their role and responsibilities in preparation for the assessment.

Note:
  For example, an assessment using a group discussion might require the assessor to facilitate and intervene to make progress and ensure that all candidates are given a fair opportunity to make their points. On the other hand, an observer role means no intervention and silent observation. (Silent observation includes absence of any behaviour that could be construed by candidates as 'leading' such as a simple smile or nodding at the wrong moment.) The assessor briefing should include advice to the candidates the level of interaction they can expect from the assessors and observers.

The workshop is your opportunity to set and manage the expectations of the assessment team, to establish your role, and to answer any questions the assessors may have. By the end of the workshop, your team should be forming into a single entity that can deliver a professional approach throughout their interactions with the candidates.

10.3.2 The Assessors toolkit

The foundation of the assessor's toolkit is the tools to do the job — the role and person specifications, the briefings, and the assessment guidance. These assist your preparation so that you know what you are looking for, rather than 'thinking' that you'll recognise a good performance when it happens!

Each assessor needs to practice and rehearse:

- Observation and listening skills, and
- Recording candidate's performance.

Observation in the context of assessment means what your assessors see and hear. An objective observation often means not showing any emotion or behaviour that could mislead the candidate as positive or negative reinforcement of what they are doing or saying.

Listening to a candidate's statements or responses to questions needs active listening. Active Listening is the technique and skill of knowing the purpose of the question and absorbing the answer without filtering the content. When listening actively, try to maintain suitable eye contact and facial expressions to demonstrate your interest in the candidate. You can also observe the candidate to see if their body language matches the answer, for example motivation and energy in the voice and body.

If you can develop the skill of waiting five to ten seconds before recording what you see and hear from candidates, it enables you to maintain and demonstrate a reasonable level of eye contact and interest while taking detailed notes.

Recording is the function of making notes while observing and listening to the candidates' responses. It requires skill and practice to be an effective recorder.

Notes can vary between verbatim notes and a sketchy summary of what was said and done. Notes may be subject to independent or external scrutiny in any appeal against non-selection so they need to accurately reflect the candidate's performance.

Electronic recording, when used in conjunction with the written notes of a candidate's performance, can be a useful backup option to support or confirm what was said or done.

It is recommended that assessors do not rely on electronic recording alone, as it can be time consuming to review a candidate's entire assessment – often more than once.

10.3.3 House rules

There are many opportunities for the assessors to collide with each other during an assessment; these collisions make the assessors look unprofessional. One element of aligning the assessor team is to the specific roles and house rules for their interactions with each other and their approach to the candidate. For example,

- Who leads with the initial introductions and gets things started?
- Which assessor asks the initial questions while the other takes notes.
- How, and when, to interject whilst keeping the flow of the assessment.
- Helping each other to remain silent and not fill a void left for the candidate.
- An agreed signal for follow-up question to gather more information.
- When to move on; make an intervention, or interact with the candidate.
- How, and when, to seamlessly handover the lead of the assessment.

Practical notes:

Interventions and Interruptions are part of the assessors' toolkit and should be deployed effectively to support the candidate, not destroy them!

An intervention might be to establish or clarify a point of interest or to summarise the your understanding of what was said. Your skills in timing an intervention or interruption is fundamental to keeping the candidate focused on the question, so that they providing evidence of competence for the role.

One assessor interrupting other assessors is unprofessional and can impact the candidate's performance as well as their perception of the organisation.

When speaking with the candidates, use impersonal pronouns such as *the candidate* rather than personal pronouns (for example *you*). For example:

Do **NOT** say, *"You are required to attend induction training events."*
Instead, say *"The successful candidate is required to attend induction training."*

This helps you to avoid the trap of tacitly offering the position. Make sure the whole project team know this important etiquette. This applies throughout the recruitment and selection process, especially in interviews.

Effective assessment
requires
Project Leadership.

10.4 Individual preparation

Individual practice is an important part of preparation for the team rehearsal and the formal assessment. You should ensure that each member the assessor team undertakes individual preparation for their role such as:

- Familiarisation with the timetable
- Practise recording information.
- Practise asking questions (speaking aloud).
- Practise the delivery of briefings (speaking aloud).
- Verifying the activity resources.
- Walking the route between activity locations.

... all of which contribute to an effective rehearsal for all the team.

10.5 Team rehearsal

10.5.1 The dress rehearsal

At this point, you have invested considerable resources into the project. The design and planning are complete; individuals have learnt their lines and practised their roles: It is time for a dress rehearsal. Rehearsals are the opportunity for the whole team to perform and coordinate their parts so that the candidate experiences a well organised and structured assessment. The rehearsal enables the assessors to familiarise themselves with the locations, the activity briefings, observing and recording.

Plan for at least one rehearsal of the whole assessment process. You should recruit a few volunteers[*] to substitute for real candidates.

> (*) To help recruit the volunteers sell the benefits for them. For example, gaining interview experience in a safe environment and feedback if they wish.
> The volunteers also provide you with valuable feedback in the review.

A rehearsal confirms that the designed assessment meets your objectives and can be achieved effectively and efficiently on the day.

10.5.2 Rehearsal and practise

The dress rehearsal includes:

- A full run-through of the assessment activity and briefings by those directly involved; test administrators, observers, note-takers.

- Testing the Logistics — dates and times, room reserved and prepared, car parking is reserved, visitor badges produced, dedicated reception space, restroom/toilet, and the provision of refreshments.

- Timing — you might be surprised about the variation of planned to actual times, especially how the movement and time between activities link with the candidate programme and assessor timetable.

- Recording the candidate evidence on the paperwork. This might be the only opportunity for you to establish consistency of observation and recording performance throughout the assessor team.

10.5.3 Review the Rehearsal

The aim of the review is to confirm:

- What worked well and what needs to be changed, if anything? For example how effective is the design at supporting your objectives?

- How well the timetable flows for the candidates and the assessors? For example, is the allocated 'downtime' for candidates and assessors sufficient for rest and recuperation, logging of notes, and refreshments?

- The instructions are clear for both the candidates and the assessors? For example, how well each briefing document meets the needs of the (volunteer) candidates and the person conducting the brief?

- The recording process of candidate performance generates the required evidence for evaluation. For example, how easy it is to observe unobtrusively, record and analyse the information acquired?

The review of the rehearsal should include the administration and assessor team plus the volunteer candidates who can provide useful feedback on the impact of the design from a candidate's perspective.

If changes are required, take care to minimise the impact on other components of the assessment and timetable. If you make extensive changes, you might need another rehearsal.

Candidates should experience the opening night; not the dress rehearsal.

11 Leading the Assessment

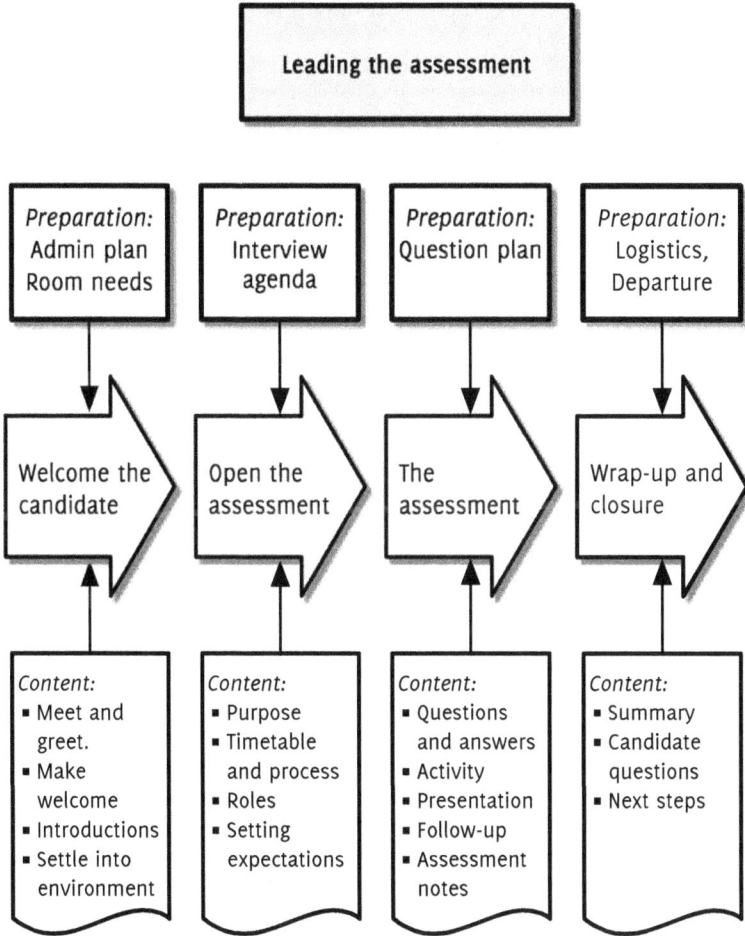

Leading the assessment

Preparation:
Admin plan
Room needs

Preparation:
Interview
agenda

Preparation:
Question plan

Preparation:
Logistics,
Departure

Welcome the
candidate

Open the
assessment

The
assessment

Wrap-up and
closure

Content:
- Meet and
  greet.
- Make
  welcome
- Introductions
- Settle into
  environment

Content:
- Purpose
- Timetable
  and process
- Roles
- Setting
  expectations

Content:
- Questions
  and answers
- Activity
- Presentation
- Follow-up
- Assessment
  notes

Content:
- Summary
- Candidate
  questions
- Next steps

Figure 15 — Leading the Assessment

11.1 The Candidate's journey of assessment

Figure 15 shows the flow of the candidate assessment. It defines the approach and sets the tone for the candidate's journey. Planning and preparation makes for an effective assessment.

Leading the assessment is the implementation of the planning and preparation — the design.

> Authors Note:
> In this Chapter the generic term assessment is used throughout to mean any assessment method (including interviews).
> The term assessor is used throughout to mean the observer, facilitator; the interviewer is an assessor.

The majority of the decisions, planning and design preparation to this point has an internal, organisational focus. The leadership and management focus now shifts directly to enabling each candidate to show what they can do and why they should be appointed.

The implementation phase, the arrows in Figure 15 reflect a typical candidate-centric agenda comprising four key elements:

- The Welcome
- Opening the assessment
- The assessment
- The Summary and Close — what next.

11.2 The Welcome

Ensure that each candidate is expected and addressed using their name and any title. This displays common courtesy and develops the candidate's overall perception of the organisation and how they as an employee might be treated.

The assessment team must be polite and professional — remember the aim is to get the best out of the candidates.

Where more than one other person is present, introduce the assessment team using their role during the assessment, for example, *"Susan is your interviewer"*, *"Peter is taking the notes"*, *"Alison is our test administrator."*

Starting a conversation using 'warm-up' questions (something the candidate is familiar with from their application) sets the tone for the assessment and is more likely to put them at ease, for example *"I see you live in [...] how long have you lived there?"* A similar approach with each candidate shows a level of interest, appears to be personal, consistent, and normally safe.

The conversation enables the candidate to be involved early in the assessment journey and is likely to relax more quickly.

11.3   Opening the assessment

Moving from the welcome, to beginning the assessment is a signal to the candidate (and the other assessors) that proceedings have started. Providing a written overview of the timetable and agenda in addition to a verbal overview generally helps to settle candidates and sets expectations for the assessment.

For example:

"Thank you for applying for the role of Marketing Manager... Today is about understanding what you have achieved and how you might contribute to the role.

During the interview, we'll be asking questions related to the role. We'll also be taking notes, so we might lose eye contact with you. When this happens, please don't stop, we're still listening."

Occasionally, we might interrupt you to clarify some information."

"At the conclusion of our 45 minute discussion there is an opportunity for you (the candidate), to ask any questions about the role or the organisation, or to add further information that might aid our decision."

If relevant, also mention activities or tests.

11.4 The assessment

A seamless transition from the welcome, agenda and timetable, to the assessment is greatly assisted by linking the candidate's application to the role for which they have applied.

> *"I see from your CV that your current role is a marketing executive... Tell me a bit about your most recent marketing campaign?"*

The statement and question links the *role* directly to the *candidate*. This synchronisation approach makes sure that both the candidate *and* the assessment team are aligned with the business of the day — the assessment.

Typically, the assessment consists of themed questions and activities so that you can:

- Confirm the candidate's skills and knowledge.
- Identify their experience reflecting their suitability for the role.
- Observe their behaviours and attitudes to assess their potential alignment with the values of the organisation.

The skill of the lead assessor is to ensure that the question and answer element of the assessment appears more conversational than inquisitional, and in so doing, observe and record evidence for the critical-few elements in the job and person specifications.

Specific questions are aimed at gaining a broad understanding of the candidate's knowledge, skills or experience. Supplementary questions get to the detail of what the candidate actually achieved or learnt.

There is value and benefit of having a secondary assessor or note-taker. The lead assessor can ask the primary and supplementary questions while demonstrating interest through active listening and eye contact. The other assessor or note-taker records the questions, the answers, and any observations.

The second assessor has the opportunity to refer to the notes to ask any further questions required to complement earlier answers, plug any gaps or areas not covered. This is a tried and tested method that additionally offers corroboration of the output that is ultimately used to assess a candidate's experience and skills.

At key points of the assessment, the lead assessor should summarise for points of clarity and to check progress. Note taking is an art in itself. The notes need to be accurate and concise for use in the summary and essential for the evaluation. Ideally, appoint a dedicated person to take the notes — this adds another pair of eyes and ears to the assessment team. (Assessors also need to take notes to identify areas to probe in their follow up questions.)

Keeping all these balls in the air can be challenging even for skilled and practiced assessors. The stakes are high: A poor recruitment can be expensive. During the assessment, it is important to remember that the assessment is primarily about the candidate and not the assessor. Remember it is difficult to assess the candidate effectively if the assessor is responsible for the majority of the input!

> The 80:20 rule —
> The assessment is about
> the candidates,
> not the assessors.

11.5 Listening to the answers

11.5.1 The purpose of active listening

Active Listening is hearing and interpreting what the candidate said in response to your question. You might need to confirm your understanding with the candidate. (Formulate a summarising question from your notes to check it was what the candidate intended.)

During the assessment, the candidate might answer a different question to the one posed. Listening actively assists you to identify what has happened and to judge whether to accept the response or to challenge the candidate in a positive manner.

Having posed a question wait silently for the candidate's response with an encouraging facial expression. Silence is a powerful tool of the assessor. If the candidate is unresponsive, resist the temptation to add extra words to the question — it is likely to confuse the candidate or to 'telegraph' an answer you are looking for.

11.5.2 Seek first-person answers

"We ..." is not an *"I"*. To assess, you need answers that relate to the personal experiences and knowledge of candidate, not the candidates colleagues or teammates. A good response from a candidate would be spoken in the first person: *"I did this,"* or *"My role was,"* and so on.

An answer in the second person *"we ..."* is a signal for two potential situations:

- The candidate is a strong team player, or
- The candidate is being evasive.

In either case, your job in the assessment is to probe and discover the candidate's individual contributions.

Candidates coming from a strong team oriented environment (and in some cultures), the candidate often responds in the second person with *"we"* meaning the activities and achievements of their team. These answers hide what the candidate actually did and make it difficult to match their individual contribution to the job and person specifications. Your role is to pursue supplementary questions (interrupting the candidate if necessary) with a directing question. For example, *"...specifically what was **your** role in the team?"* (Verbally stressing the *"your"* should signal to the candidate to re-orient their response.)

For example:

Assessor, *"Tell me about your role in the marketing office?"*

Candidate, *"What we did was to put key messages ... "*

Assessor, interrupting *"Yes, but what was **your** job?"*

Candidate, *"The importance of the campaign was to persuade ..."*

This candidate is being evasive. If unchecked, this loop might continue with no evidence to record. Time is precious so you have to think on your feet, and change the approach. In this example strong directing questions are used to discover the where the candidate fits in their team.

Assessor, *"Ok, so I can understand how things work, briefly **describe** the step-by-step process of the campaign?"* (A gentle directing question.)

The candidate describes the steps from editorial, printing, and distribution.

Assessor, *"So, to summarise the steps are 1 ... 2 ... [through to] 5.... Which step did **you** work in?"* (Closed question.)

Candidate, *"I worked in step 5."*

Assessor, *"Good, thank you. Would **you tell me precisely** what **you** did in step 5?"* (A strong directing question.)

The interviewer discovered that the candidate's former team stuffed flyers into envelopes. The candidate's role was to put the stamps on the envelopes and place them in an out-tray.

11.5.3 Hypothetical responses

A candidate's answer that includes the phrase, *"I think"* is acceptable in hypothetical situations where you are trying to assess their thought processing, logic, or creativity. If similar *"I think"* responses were given as you attempt to establish evidence of competence, then supplementary questions would be needed to probe and investigate the candidate's expertise.

11.5.4 Hooks and supplementary questions

The candidate's answers might contain hooks for supplementary questions that enable the assessor to probe deeper for further evidence.

Example:

Assessor: *"What is it that you most enjoy in your current role?"*

Candidate: *"...I like the responsibility and making my own decisions."*

Two 'hooks' have been offered: *responsibilities* and to *own decisions*. You could move on to the next question on the prepared list (and miss the opportunity to discover more about your candidate) or ask supplementary questions following up the hooks to discover the more evidence.

Assessor: *"That's interesting, tell me about the responsibilities you have?"*

Further evidence about the individual's level and extent of responsibilities is discovered.

Assessor: *"Give me some examples of the decisions you made?"*

Depending on the response to this supplementary question....

Assessor: *"How (or Why) did you go about making that decision?"*

... and then a supplementary question:

Assessor: *"What was the impact of that decision on your customers/ colleagues/stakeholders/ ... ?"*

By asking supplementary questions, you can gain more detail and insights about the candidate's leadership style, and whether the candidate is self-aware of the consequences of how the decision was made and what it was. Remember too, that when you have sufficient evidence you can move on to another topic.

11.6   Closing the assessment

Bringing the assessment to a natural closure helps you to set and manage candidate expectations and an overall positive perception of the organisation.

There are at least six steps to this closure:

- Verify any incomplete information, and offer your candidate an opportunity to add or clarify any points.

- Ask any colleagues, if they have anything additional to ask the candidate.

- Ask if the candidate if they have anything else to add that has not been covered that could help you in the your evaluation.

- Offer the candidate the opportunity to ask any questions they might have about the role.

  Note:
  The lead assessor should respond openly and honestly, avoiding any direct reference to the candidate's performance, and by confirming only general information or next steps such as the timing of the decision and appointment.

- The lead assessor brings closure to the interview by thanking the candidate for their time and interest in the role.

- Escort your candidate courteously to their next on-site location or departure point.

  Note:
  Assessment days can be very stressful and a duty of care to your candidates would be to ensure they are safe to leave your premises.

12 Leading the evaluation

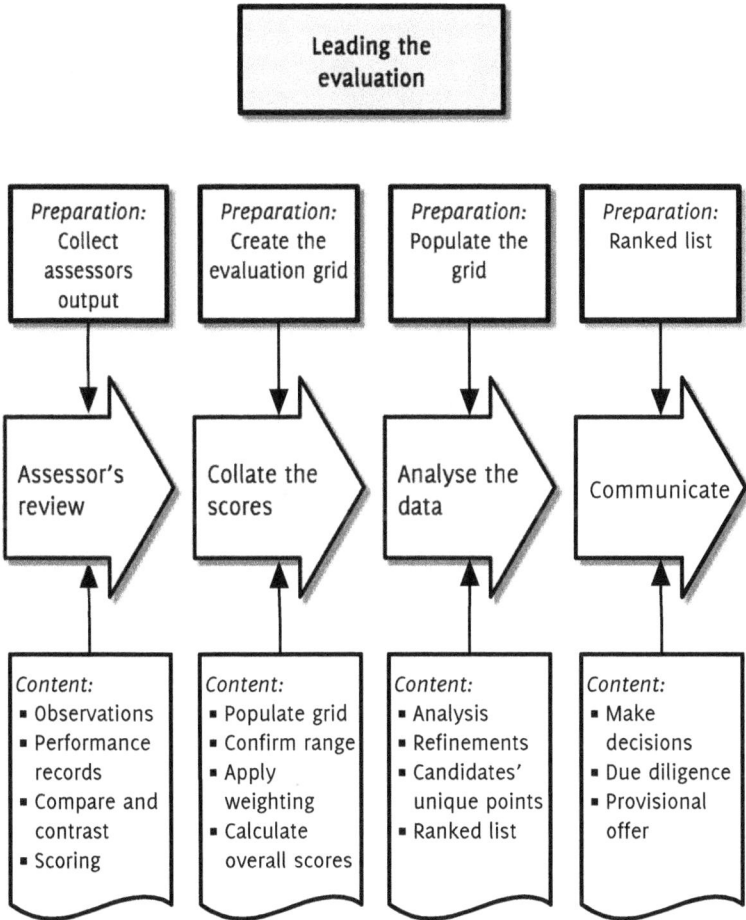

Figure 16 — Leading the evaluation

Evaluation is the culmination of the candidate assessment. It enables you to judge the performance or competence of each candidate against each criterion for the competence.

The purpose of evaluation is to provide you with a ranked list of candidates who can fulfil the role.

12.1 Evaluating your candidates

There are three steps to leading the evaluation of your candidates:

- A post-assessment meeting with the assessors to share their observations and experience. Assessors score by comparing and contrasting the candidate's performance for each activity against the criterion for the role. Collect the performance records and scores for each candidate plus any additional evidence that might be useful during your subsequent analysis.

- Collate the candidate scores by transferring them to the evaluation grid you created. Validate the scores are within the agreed range for each criterion. Apply the weighting factors to generate an overall score for each candidate, and an initial numerical ranking.

- Refine your analysis further by reviewing candidate specific achievements for each activity. This secondary analysis might simply provide confirmation of the numerical ranking. It might however, provide you with an insight to skills, knowledge, or differentiation that could be useful to the organisation and prove helpful in the final evaluation.

Once the analysis of the data is complete and you are satisfied that the best candidates also reflect the values and culture of the organisation it is time to make your decision.

An example:

Based on their application and CV, a candidate was invited to attend a two-day assessment centre for an international leisure company.

The candidate performed highly in the majority of the assessment activities and the subsequent numerical evaluation placed him ahead of other candidates on the ranked list.

In the analysis phase, several of the assessors reported observations that the candidate's personal behaviour was not that of a team player. Despite the high scores on other factors, the organisation was unable to risk appointing that candidate.

Learning points for the company included:

- The importance of the role *and* the person specification in successful recruitment.

- The essential criteria must be stated clearly in the marketing of the role and weighted in the final evaluation.

- The value of matching the assessment activities to the role.

Numerical evaluation alone is not a sufficient analysis.

12.2 The offer

12.2.1 The provisional offer

Once you have made your decision and confirmed your choice of candidate — do not delay in contacting your intended employee to make the offer.

The usual approach is for you to advise the successful candidate as soon as practicable after the evaluation. Ideally, make a personal telephone call, to confirm that they are still interested in being recruited! It would be unfortunate if you were to lose their interest now, after all the effort expended to get this far.

12.2.2 Due Diligence

Due diligence is establishing what you can about an individual's background information prior to employment, to minimise risks to your organisation.

Historically, written references from former employers were considered a good measure of a person's character, the quality of their work, their work ethic and reliability. However, in recent years references have become simply a statement of limited facts for example, *"Mrs X was employed between (date) and (date) in the role of..."* The references might confirm other information — assuming it does not contravene data protection and confidentiality laws.

Recently, due diligence could be individuals acting as referees who vouch for your candidate. Additionally, it might involve detailed background checks, for example, a work permit, an entry visa, professional society membership, criminal record, or qualification. The need for due diligence varies by the role, your industry sector, and jurisdiction.

Caveat emptor — it is 'buyer beware' when it comes to references, however, as the new employer it is more important that you implement an effective induction and orientation programme to monitor the new employees performance during a defined probation period.

13 Feedback

13.1 Feedback to successful candidates

Once the candidate has accepted the role and become an employee, an early part of their induction should be feedback from their performance in the selection process. It is easy for you to administer and leads your new employee's expectations through their early period of employment.

To ensure that the feedback has meaning and value beyond the selection, it should be:

- open and honest,
- factual regarding what was said or did, that secured the role for them, and
- identify any gaps requiring training or development.

13.2 Feedback for unsuccessful candidates

Many organisations simply invoke a minimal feedback policy. For example, the well-worn and empty phrase *'other candidates were better suited to the position.'*

Unsuccessful candidates undoubtedly talk to others about their experience of you, your organisation, and your recruitment process. Unsuccessful candidates have great potential to enhance, (or damage), your reputation. The benefit of providing feedback to unsuccessful candidates is to maintain their positive perception of your organisation as a possible future employer.

The time taken to offer feedback that helps candidates with future applications to your organisation or others is a good way to promote your organisation with those who were not successful.

14 Project Closure

14.1 Why close the project

Your recruitment and selection project has reached a successful conclusion. With the job offered and the start date confirmed, the project has now fulfilled the promise declared in the PID. It is now time to hand-over the new employee to their line management, transferring ownership of the subsequent induction, training, and integration into business as usual.

Closing a project makes sure that it doesn't linger on; it informs the stakeholders that the job is done, and formally releases the various resources to work on other projects.

14.2 How to close the project

Closing the project means arranging an end of project review meeting of those involved. Make it a meeting that people want to attend and gain extra credibility for leading and managing an effective meeting too.

- Establish a sense of personal and team achievement. Recognise new experiences, skills, and knowledge — add these to personal development plans or CV.

- Use the PID as the basis for reviewing the project by comparing what actually happened against what was expected.

- Focus initially on the project elements that specifically contributed to a successful project. Record what was learnt that should be repeated in future. What should you do differently next time? What project trade-offs did you make?

- Identify and record what benefits were achieved. What benefits were expected? Were there any surprises? How are you measuring the benefits?

- Evaluate the overall investment and the return on that investment.

- Create a 'project closure statement' — this document summarises and communicates what was achieved. It records and shares the benefits and the learning. (The purpose statement from the PID is helpful for this). You might want to create a customised version for the project owner.

- Gain personal credibility — enhance your reputation for leading and managing a recruitment and selection project to a successful conclusion.

At the end of the project,
celebrate
the team's success.

Appendix 1 — Protecting your brand

In terms of public relations, if you have five hundred applications, you have five hundred people who could speak positively about your organisation. Don't waste that opportunity! Throughout your project, take care to design-in those positive experiences.

Table 14 — Typical factors determining the candidate's satisfaction

Positive experience (Brand enhancing)	Negative experience (Brand damaging)
The invitation: Quality information about the event, timetable, directions, car parking, and location of reception.	Poor quality information about the event. Left to own devices. Feels like an initiative test.
On arrival: refreshment in a dedicated reception room, visitor badge with correct name, and a host.	If arriving early — left in a cold, desolate waiting room — no refreshment and no company.
Welcome is friendly, courteous, Introductions to everyone involved.	Welcome is cold or clinical.
Room with natural light, water, small coffee table, and a comfortable chair.	Dark room, poor lighting, a panel of inquisitors, uncomfortable chair.
Assessments: Engaging, conversational, clarity.	Straight to the facts, inquisition.
Relevant questions, matched to the application form or cv and follow-up questions related to the previous answers.	Several or multiple questions with no obvious links to the previous question or response.
No disruptions, linked and relevant activities, no waiting between activities.	Disruptions, distractions, and time wasting between activities.
Farewell — hosted back to Reception.	Dismissed and left to own devices.

Additional Resources

Resources and other titles in the Leadership Library, are available online.
Point your browser to www.leadership-library.co.uk
The QR code takes you to the same page.

Free or inexpensive files to accompany this book are downloadable for use without restrictions, and are available in common industry standard file formats, including Microsoft Office, and Rich Text Format (.rtf).

Project Initiation Document: An example PID — which can be adapted to suit your specific requirements.

Evaluation Spreadsheet: A common method of keeping track of the assessments during sifting and selection elements of recruitment and selection.

Induction and orientation: The first day, and the first week set the tone and expectations for a new recruit. This resource includes a timetable and checklist that help you and the recruit to settle in and start being productive.

Bespoke resources: If you have a need for bespoke resources please let us know via email to editor@leadership-library.co.uk
Resources related to recruitment and selection include:

- Customised versions of this book incorporating your own company's procedures and branding.

- Developing project leadership, through seminars or training.

- Facilitating project team kick-off workshops.

- Interview skills for staff development.

LL-el144633as

About the authors

Eddie Lunn — In a career spanning thirty-five years with an international communications company, he was the driving force for senior leadership development programmes involving over five thousand managers. Eddie is a former member of the Chartered Management Institute, (CMI), the British Psychological Society, (BPS), and holds a Masters degree in Business Administration

Alan Sarsby — has enjoyed over forty years in many different careers; initially in electronic engineering and IT strategy, then later in customer service, quality, and business change. He has developed and implemented unique approaches to enterprise design and change leadership. He is a Member of the Institute of Engineering and Technology (MIET) and holds the degree of Bachelor of Technology (hons.).

Alan and Eddie have considerable experience and work together on many training events. Customers include commercial, industrial, voluntary, public sector, and not-for-profit sectors.

Acknowledgement

The authors wish to acknowledge that earlier work developed in collaboration with Pietro Bisset, has contributed to this book.

Leadership
Library

www.ingramcontent.com/pod-product-compliance
Lightning Source LLC
Chambersburg PA
CBHW071203200326
41519CB00018B/5352